8/98

P9-BJO-481

EMPLOYEE RIGHTS IN THE WORKPLACE

by
Margaret C. Jasper, Esq.

Oceana's Legal Almanac Series:
Law for the Layperson

1997
Oceana Publications, Inc.
Dobbs Ferry, N.Y.

Information contained in this work has been obtained by Oceana Publications from sources believed to be reliable. However, neither the Publisher nor its authors guarantee the accuracy or completeness of any information published herein, and neither Oceana nor its authors shall be responsible for any errors, omissions or damages arising from the use of this information. This work is published with the understanding that Oceana and its authors are supplying information, but are not attempting to render legal or other professional services. If such services are required, the assistance of an appropriate professional should be sought.

You may order this or any other Oceana publications by visiting Oceana's website at http:\\www.oceanalaw.com

ISBN: 0-379-11243- 4 (alk. paper: acid-free paper)

Manufactured in the United States of America on acid-free paper.

To My Husband Chris

Your love and support
are my motivation and inspiration

—and—

In memory of my son, Jimmy

ABOUT THE AUTHOR

MARGARET C. JASPER is an attorney engaged in the general practice of law in South Salem, New York, concentrating in the areas of personal injury and entertainment law. Ms. Jasper holds a Juris Doctor degree from Pace University School of Law, White Plains, New York, is a member of the New York and Connecticut bars, and is certified to practice before the United States District Courts for the Southern and Eastern Districts of New York, and the United States Supreme Court.

Ms. Jasper has been appointed to the panel of arbitrators of the American Arbitration Association and the law guardian panel for the Family Court of the State of New York, and is a New York State licensed real estate broker and member of the Westchester County Board of Realtors, operating as Jasper Real Estate, in South Salem, New York.

Ms. Jasper is the author and general editor of the following legal almanacs: Juvenile Justice and Children's Law; Marriage and Divorce; Estate Planning; The Law of Contracts; The Law of Dispute Resolution; Law for the Small Business Owner; The Law of Personal Injury; Real Estate Law for the Homeowner and Broker; Everyday Legal Forms; Dictionary of Selected Legal Terms; The Law of Medical Malpractice; The Law of Product Liability; The Law of No-Fault Insurance; The Law of Immigration; The Law of Libel and Slander; The Law of Buying and Selling; Elder Law; The Right to Die; AIDS Law; Obscenity, Pornography and the Law; The Law of Child Custody; The Law of Debt Collection; Consumer Rights Law; Bankruptcy Law for the Individual Debtor; Victim's Rights Law; Animal Rights Law and Workers' Compensation Law.

TABLE OF CONTENTS

INTRODUCTION

This almanac attempts to give the reader an overview of the rights an individual is entitled to in the workplace. It provides relevant information on the most common employment-related issues. It is important that the individual become familiar with his or her rights because it is less likely that an informed employee will be taken advantage of by their employer.

For example, the average citizen works so that they have money to pay for their housing and necessities, and put food on the table. Of course, job satisfaction is a priority, but it is generally meaningless if one cannot support their family. Thus, an overriding concern of the average worker is that they be paid fairly for the work they perform.

Unfortunately, this is not always the case. For this reason, both federal and state governments have enacted statutes to protect workers in this regard. As further set forth in this almanac, the most comprehensive statute regulating fair pay and related practices is *The Fair Labor Standards Act.*

In addition to concerns about fair pay, most workers have other questions concerning fair treatment in their workplace, particularly if an employment-related problem arises. For example, an employee may suspect that his age was the reason he was passed over for a promotion. An applicant may believe that her disability was the reason she was not hired in the first place.

Many uninformed individuals will simply overlook these forms of discrimination because they don't believe there is anything they can do about it. However, this treatment does not have to be tolerated. In fact, it should be addressed and dealt with so that employers are given the message that they will be challenged and punished for engaging in discriminatory behavior.

For this reason, major federal legislation has been enacted which is designed to protect individuals from discrimination based on such factors as age, gender, disability, race or national origin. A discussion of these major federal laws, such as *The Civil Rights Act*; *The Americans with Disabilities* Act; and *The Age Discrimination in Employment Act*, is set forth in this almanac.

Workers are also very concerned about losing their job if they take time off due to serious health concerns, either for themselves or their family, or in connection with the birth or adoption of a child. This almanac discusses the *Family Medical and Leave Act*, which recognizes that there are legitimate reasons an individual may need to take a leave from work, without fear of retaliation or loss of employment.

This almanac also addresses other workplace concerns, such as health and safety, privacy issues and sexual harassment. The Appendix provides sample forms, applicable statutes, and other pertinent information and data. The Glossary contains definitions of many of the terms used throughout the almanac.

CHAPTER 1:
PRESERVING YOUR RIGHTS IN THE WORKPLACE

Maintaining a Personal Employment File

Preserving your rights in the workplace begins from the moment you are hired as an employee. Every employee should make it a practice to keep a personal employment file which documents their entire relationship with their employer. Although it is difficult to anticipate a problem in the workplace, it is much more difficult to prevail in a lawsuit if there is no documentation to support one's grievances.

EXAMPLE: After years of glowing performance evaluations, a minority employee in a large chain store is suddenly fired after a new manager is put in charge of the department. The employee believes that he was fired because the new manager is a racist — an unlawful motive for dismissal. In fact, he has overheard the manager make racially biased remarks about minority customers to co-workers.

When he asked why he was dismissed, the employee was told that he was incapable of meeting the requirements of the position — a position he has held for the past three years. The employee points out that he received extremely high ratings on all of his past performance evaluations. The employee is told that there is no record of these evaluations in the employee's personnel folder.

The employee decides to bring a lawsuit against the employer. In support of his claim, he is asked to provide copies of the performance evaluations. Unfortunately, the employee did not keep copies of any of these evaluations. The result — the employee has only his word against the employer to prove he was a highly capable worker, and that the stated reason for his dismissal was merely a pretext for the real motive, i.e., the manager's racial bias.

The employee further claims that he has overheard the manager make racially biased remarks about minority customers on a number of occasions. Unfortunately, he cannot remember exactly when the comments were made, the exact words used, or the names of the other employees present at the time.

Without corroboration from co-workers, there is little to bolster this employee's claims. Often, co-workers do not want to get involved for fear that they will also lose their jobs. Again, it is his word against the employer.

If the employee had kept his performance evaluations for the past three years, it would certainly raise a valid question as to how the employee's evaluation could have plummeted so drastically after the new manager was hired.

In addition, it is advisable to keep a journal to document any unusual or significant events that occur in the workplace, including the basic facts, e.g., date, time, place, statements made, actions taken, and persons present, etc.

If the employee in the above example had kept a journal detailing events which occurred at the workplace, there would be entries made concerning the date, time and witnesses to the manager's biased remarks. This would certainly weigh in favor of the employee's claim of discrimination.

Therefore, one should not wait until a problem arises in the workplace to start accumulating evidence. All work-related documents, including employee handbooks, performance evaluations, and memorandums, etc., should be kept in the employee's personal employment file.

Alternative Dispute Resolution

Problems which arise in the workplace do not always have to end up in litigation. Some problems can be worked out using alternative dispute resolution methods. For example, the employee can try and work the problem out directly with the employer by arranging an informal meeting. The employee may also use mediation, or the more formal arbitration process to avoid litigation.

Private Negotiation

The most informal method of alternative dispute resolution would be for the employee to arrange a private meeting with his or her employer to openly discuss the problem. Most employers would rather avoid a lawsuit if a legitimate grievance is brought to their attention. If the employee is a member of a union, the union representative may attend the meeting to help informally mediate any disputes.

In order to adequately prepare for this meeting, one must be knowledgeable about his or her legal rights concerning the specific problem, e.g. discrimination, harassment, unfair pay, etc, including the possible sanctions available to the employee under the law.

The employee should calmly and intelligently set forth the basic facts surrounding the conflict, and explain how the employee's rights were thereby violated. This demonstrates to the employer that the employee is serious about pursuing legal action.

Mediation

Mediation is also used in settling employer/employee disputes where the parties are generally on good terms and willing to mediate the dispute. In such a case, the more formal process of arbitration, as set forth below, is not considered necessary unless an impasse occurs in the mediation process.

Mediation, like arbitration, enlists the assistance of a neutral third party, known as a mediator. However, the role of the mediator differs from that of the arbitrator. The mediator does not issue a binding decision but rather assists the opposing parties in resolving their own dispute, which resolution may then be formalized in a written agreement. The mediator cannot force the parties to change their positions. Thus, the parties remain responsible for negotiating a settlement of their dispute.

Arbitration

Many employers have turned to arbitration to resolve employer/employee disputes when the less formal methods of alternative dispute resolution have failed and litigation is seen as a last resort.

Arbitration is an expedient and cost effective way in which to settle a controversy, and gives the parties a sense of control over the process because they can actively participate in the negotiation and settlement of the dispute. In addition, arbitration offers the advantage of permitting the parties to hire an arbitrator who has knowledge of the operations of the particular industry. Further, a lawsuit is generally a matter of public record, whereas arbitration is a private and confidential proceeding.

Litigation is time consuming. It can go on for many years while the parties exhaust all of their appellate remedies. Arbitration provides an expeditious resolution of the dispute, particularly since the awards are binding and final. The parties generally have no right to appeal the arbitrator's decision.

Litigation is expensive. Expenses may include legal fees and disbursements, court filing fees and costs, expert witness fees, investigation costs, etc. Most employees do not have the resources to keep a lawsuit going, particularly if they are up against a major corporate employer. On the other hand, the cost of arbitration is generally predictable and comparatively small.

Last Resort: Litigation

Once the employee has exhausted all of his or her nonjudicial remedies without satisfaction, he or she may consider taking legal action. It is important, however, to outline exactly what one expects or desires to gain by bringing a lawsuit, and whether it will be worth the time and expense. Of course, if the employer's actions were particularly outrageous, it may be reason enough to bring legal action on principle alone.

Relatively minor grievances may not result in a recovery that warrants litigation. In addition, as discussed above, if the employee cannot document his or her case sufficiently, the chances of prevailing in the lawsuit are slight. All of these factors should be reviewed with one's attorney before proceeding with litigation.

A more detailed discussion of alternative dispute resolution may be found in this author's almanac entitled *The Law of Dispute Resolution* also published by Oceana Publishing Company.

CHAPTER 2:
EMPLOYMENT DISCRIMINATION

In General

Employment discrimination refers to the illegal practice of making employment decisions, such as hiring and promotion, based on an employee's age, race, sex, religion, national origin, or physical disability. There are a number of state and federal laws which prohibit discrimination in the workplace. Different types of employers are subject to different laws, as more fully described below.

State and Federal Government Employers

The Fifth and Fourteenth Amendments to the United States Constitution also limit the power of the federal and state governments to discriminate in employment. For example, the Fifth Amendment forbids the federal government from depriving any individual of life, liberty or property without due process of law, and further requires that there be equal protection under the law. The Fourteenth Amendment makes the prohibitions contained in the Fifth Amendment applicable to the states.

Therefore, state and federal government employers are constitutionally prohibited from treating employees differently, e.g. based upon race or gender.

Private Sector

Private employers, as well as state and local governments and public or private educational institutions, employment agencies, labor unions, and apprentice programs are subject to the anti-discrimination laws listed below. The private sector, however, is not directly prohibited by the constitutional provisions discussed above.

Federal Anti-Discrimination Laws

The Equal Employment Opportunity Commission (EEOC) was established by Title VII of the Civil Rights Act of 1964. The EEOC interprets and enforces the major federal anti-discrimination laws, including (i) Title VII of the Civil Rights Act of 1964; (ii) The Americans with Disabilities Act of 1990 (ADA); and (iii) The Age Discrimination in Employment Act (ADEA) of 1967.

A summary of the major anti-discrimination statutes is set forth below.

Title VII of the Civil Rights Act of 1964

Title VII of the Civil Rights Act of 1964, as amended, prohibits discrimination in hiring, promotion, discharge, pay, fringe benefits, and other aspects of employment, on the basis of race, color, religion, sex, or national origin. Most private employers, state and local governments, educational institutions, employment agencies, and labor organizations are subject to Title VII, which covers both current employees and job applicants.

The 19th Century Civil Rights Act, which was amended in 1993, ensures that all persons are afforded equal rights under the law. The Act sets forth the damages available to prevailing plaintiffs in actions brought under the Civil Rights Act of 1964,

The Americans with Disabilities Act of 1990

The Americans with Disabilities Act (ADA) prohibits discrimination against individuals with "qualified" disabilities as set forth in the statute. The Act generally applies to government employers and private sector employers who engage in interstate commerce.

The ADA is more fully discussed in Chapter 3 of this Almanac.

The Age Discrimination in Employment Act of 1967

Age discrimination in employment is governed by the Age Discrimination in Employment Act (the "ADEA"), as amended. The ADEA prohibits employers from discriminating against individuals over 40 on account of their age. The statute pertains to federal, state and local employers, as well as private employers provided they employ 20 or more employees. Unions and employment agencies are also subject to the ADEA provided they meet certain criteria.

The ADEA is more fully discussed in Chapter 4 of this Almanac.

Suspected violations of the anti-discrimination laws should be reported to the United States Equal Employment Opportunity Commission (EEOC) located at 1801 L Street, N.W., Washington, DC 20507. An EEOC field office can be located by calling 800-669-EEOC. Individuals who are hearing impaired may dial the EEOC's TDD number, 800-800-3302.

State Employment Discrimination Statutes

Many state statutes provide additional protection against employment discrimination. Some of these laws are patterned after the federal statutes, and provide similar protection to workers employed by those employers not covered under the federal statutes. Some state laws also extend protection to additional groups not covered by the federal laws. Thus, the reader is advised to check the laws of his or her own jurisdiction.

Discrimination in Employment of Aliens

The Supreme Court has applied a strict scrutiny test to restrictions imposed on employment of aliens. For example, it has invalidated state laws which seek to ban aliens from civil service positions, unless an important governmental function is served by a particular position, e.g. a state trooper.

Nevertheless, the Supreme Court has stated that federal restrictions on employment of aliens would likely be upheld as an exercise of the federal government's power over immigration and foreign policy, and a legitimate expression of national interest.

Private employers are prohibited by the Civil Rights Act of 1964 from discriminating on the basis of race, national origin, or religion. However, the Act does not prohibit the employer from favoring citizens over aliens in employment decisions.

The Immigration Reform and Control Act of 1990 (IRCA) is a mechanism by which illegal immigration is controlled through the employment system. The IRCA, which is governed by the United States Immigration and Naturalization Service (INS), requires public and private employers to determine that each person hired is legally authorized to work. The IRCA is comprised of two parts—the anti-discrimination provision and the employer sanction provision.

Anti-Discrimination Provision

The anti-discrimination provision prohibits employment discrimination based on national origin and citizenship status and requires that employers treat all job applicants equally. It specifically prohibits employers from discriminating in hiring against citizens, permanent residents, temporary residents conferred legalized status under IRCA, refugees and asylees. Thus, an employer may bar the hiring of an alien only if the alien is not protected under IRCA.

Employers who violate this provision, or retaliate against employees who file discrimination charges, are subject to monetary sanctions ranging up to $2,000 per individual for the first offense, up to $5,000 per individual for the second offense, and up to $10,000 per individual for subsequent offenses.

Employer Sanctions Provision

The employer sanctions provision is concerned with the hiring of undocumented workers. Under this provision, employers must complete IRS Form I-9, which is used to verify the employment eligibility and identity of employees.

Individuals who were employed prior to November 6, 1986 are not subject to the IRCA, and the employer cannot be penalized for retaining those employees, even if they are illegal aliens. The IRCA imposes the same monetary sanctions against employers who violate the employer sanction provision as those who violate the anti-discrimination provision.

A more detailed discussion of immigration law may be found in this author's legal almanac entitled *The Law of Immigration*, also published by Oceana Publishing Company.

CHAPTER 3:
DISABILITY DISCRIMINATION

In General

It is recognized that disabled persons are a source of great talent and ability, and employment of such individuals results in tremendous benefits to our society. Unfortunately, to our detriment, because of bias, insensitivity and plain ignorance, this vast resource has been virtually excluded from meaningful participation in the workforce. This is generally known as disability discrimination—the illegal practice of making employment decisions affecting an employee based upon his or her disability.

Acknowledging that disabled persons are entitled to civil rights protections such as those already provided to individuals who are discriminated against on the basis of race, color, sex, national origin, age, and religion, the federal government intervened to provide disabled persons with effective legislation to enforce their civil rights.

The Rehabilitation Act

Prior to the passage of the ADA, recourse for disability discrimination was mainly sought under Section 503 of the Rehabilitation Act of 1973. Section 503 prohibits job discrimination because of handicaps. Section 503 also requires affirmative action by the employer to employ and advance qualified individuals with handicaps who, with reasonable accommodation, can perform the essential functions of a job.

The Americans with Disabilities Act

In 1990, members of the U.S. Congress passed a piece of legislation known as the Americans with Disabilities Act (ADA). This law provides for equal opportunity for all persons in the areas of employment, public services and accommodations, and telecommunications.

As it relates to employment issues, the ADA prohibits discrimination in all employment practices, including job application procedures, hiring, firing, compensation, advancement, and other terms and conditions of employment and related activities. Most private employers, state and local governments, educational institutions, employment agencies, and labor organizations are subject to the ADA.

Persons covered under the ADA are defined as "qualified" individuals with disabilities. A disabled person is defined as a person who has a physical or mental impairment that substantially limits one or more major life activities. Covered infirmities range from paraplegia to AIDS. Minor impairments would not likely be included under the ADA.

In addition, persons who are discriminated against because they know, are associated with, or are related to a disabled individual are also protected. This provision was included to protect individuals from actions based on a misguided belief that a relationship with a disabled person would affect the individual's ability to perform the job.

For example, if an employee's parent is suffering from a terminal illness, it is unjust to presume that the employee will miss too much time from work as a result of caring for their family member.

This provision also protects employees from adverse action caused by bias or ignorance concerning certain disabilities. For example, if an employee's family member suffers from a disease, such as AIDS, he or she should not suffer job discrimination due to the ignorant assumption that AIDS can be transmitted through casual contact.

Qualified

To be "qualified," the individual must meet the requirements of the position and be able to perform the "essential functions" of the position, with or without "reasonable accommodations." This includes applicants for employment and employees.

Essential Functions

The law requires that the disabled individual must be able to perform the "essential" functions of the job. The term "essential" was used so that individuals would not be deemed unqualified merely because they are unable to perform incidental or inconsequential tasks related to the position.

Further, if the individual is qualified to perform the essential job functions, except for certain limitations caused by their disability, the employer is obliged to consider whether the individual could perform these functions if "reasonable accommodations" are provided.

Reasonable Accommodations

The guidelines promulgated by the Equal Employment Opportunity Commission (EEOC) provide that an employer must make a reasonable effort to provide an appropriate reasonable accommodation for a qualified disabled employee who requests one.

A reasonable accommodation is any modification or adjustment to the work environment that will enable a qualified disabled individual to perform the essential job functions. For example, a wheel-chair bound employee may request that his or her work hours begin and end before or after rush hour to facilitate travel.

If the employee is unable to perform the "essential functions" of his or her position—and there are no reasonable accommodations which would enable the employee to function in that position—a reasonable accommodation may include reassignment to another available position.

If an employer fails to make a "reasonable accommodation" for a disabled employee, this may constitute a violation of the ADA. Nevertheless, an employer is not required to provide a reasonable accommodation that would pose an undue hardship on the business.

An "undue hardship" is defined as an "action requiring significant difficulty or expense" when considered in light of a number of factors, such as the nature and cost of the accommodation in relation to the resources of the employer. For example, a large employer with greater resources would be expected to make more extensive accommodations than would be required of a smaller employer.

In addition, the employer does not have to hire an individual who poses a direct threat or significant risk of substantial harm to his or her health or safety, or the health and safety of others, if that risk cannot be eliminated or significantly reduced by means of a reasonable accommodation.

In any event, the employer must substantiate that the risk is real and not merely a perceived threat, e.g. by objective medical evidence.

Further, an employer is not required to find a disabled employee alternative employment if it is not reasonably available. In that case, the disabled employee would not be "qualified" because he or she does not meet the requirements of the position, and is unable to perform the essential functions of the position, with or without a reasonable accommodation.

The law does not, however, require the employer to give the disabled applicant any preferential treatment over other applicants. Employers are free to select the most qualified applicant available provided those decisions are based on reasons unrelated to the disability.

Medical Examinations

Prior to making a job offer, an employer is not permitted to make a job applicant submit to a medical examination. However, this prohibition does not apply to testing for illegal drug use. Individuals who use illegal drugs are excluded from the definition of a "qualified" individual with a disability, and thus not protected by the ADA.

On the other hand, an individual suffering from alcoholism is considered a person with a disability protected by the ADA, provided he or she is qualified to perform the essential functions of the job. Nevertheless, the employer is free to fire or otherwise discipline an alcoholic employee if their addiction adversely affects their job performance or conduct. The employer can further require that the alcoholic employee refrain from drinking alcohol while on the job.

Further, an employer cannot make any pre-employment inquiry into the extent of an individual's disability. The employer may, however, inquire into the ability of the employee to perform the essential functions of the job.

Employment may be conditioned upon a satisfactory medical examination once the job offer is made, provided that this requirement is made of all applicants. If the results of the medical examination reveal a disability, the employer must hire the individual unless the disability is employment-related, and no reasonable accommodations are available that would enable the applicant to perform the essential functions of the position.

Bringing a Disability Discrimination Claim under the ADA

The employment provisions of the ADA are enforced under the same procedures now applicable to race, color, sex, national origin, and religious discrimination under Title VII of the Civil Rights Act of 1964, as amended, and the Civil Rights Act of 1991. Complaints may be filed with the Equal Employment Opportunity Commission or the designated state human rights agency.

When seeking to litigate an anti-discrimination claim, one must: (i) be a "qualified individual" with a recognized disability and (ii) have suffered an adverse employment decision. However, meeting these two criteria does not guarantee that the individual will prevail on his or her claim.

An employer has the right to discharge or otherwise sanction a disabled employee for any reason other than for discriminatory reasons. Disability discrimination is very dependent upon the facts of each situation. Thus, it is crucial that the individual document the facts surrounding the alleged discriminatory act.

One is also advised to seek consultation with a lawyer experienced in this area so that any legitimate claims may be presented in a timely fashion. Certain statutes have time requirements which must be met or the claim will be barred.

For example, in order to obtain the right to sue in federal or state court, an individual must first file a discrimination claim with the EEOC. Usually, the claim must be filed within 180 days of the alleged act of discrimination. A different time limit may apply if there is a state agency which oversees discrimination claims.

The reader is advised to check the law of his or her own jurisdiction concerning time limitations. A claim which is not filed within the required time period will likely be barred.

Under the ADA, if the individual decides to proceed with a civil lawsuit against the employer, the action must be filed within ninety days after receipt of the EEOC "right to sue" letter.

An individual who prevails in his or her discrimination claim under the ADA is generally entitled to recover the following: (i) the economic losses that would have been earned if the discrimination had not taken place, e.g. promotion, back pay, front pay, benefits; (ii) reasonable accommodations; (iii) damages for emotional trauma and any associated physical suffering; and (iv) attorney fees and costs.

In addition, compensatory and punitive damages may also be available in cases of intentional discrimination or where an employer fails to make a good faith effort to provide a reasonable accommodation.

Because state law may provide even greater compensation to the victim, the reader is again advised to check the law of his or her jurisdiction in this regard.

Relevant employment-related provisions of the Americans With Disabilities Act are set forth in the Appendix.

The President's Committee on Employment of People with Disabilities

In General

The President's Committee on Employment of People with Disabilities is a small federal agency whose chairman and vice-chairs are appointed by the President. The Chairman appoints the other Executive Board members and members of the six standing subcommittees. Directed by the Chairman and Executive Board, the Committee achieves its goals through the work of its subcommittee members and a 37-member agency staff, in close cooperation with the Governor's Committees in the states, Puerto Rico and Guam.

A Directory of State Governor's Committees on Employment of People with Disabilities is set forth in the Appendix.

Mission

The stated mission of the Committee is to facilitate the communication, coordination and promotion of public and private efforts to enhance the employment of people with disabilities. The Committee provides information, training, and technical assistance to America's business leaders, organized labor, rehabilitation and service providers, advocacy organizations, and families and individuals with disabilities. The President's Committee reports to the President on the progress and problems of maximizing employment opportunities for people with disabilities.

Projects

As part of their initiative, the President's Committee has developed the projects summarized below.

The Workforce Recruitment Program

The Workforce Recruitment Program maintains a database of college students with disabilities. The students are available on a full-time or part-time basis. They come from more than 140 colleges and universities, and include graduate and law students.

Each year, recruiters interview about 1,000 students with disabilities at colleges and university campuses across the nation for listing in the database.

The Business Leadership Network

The Business Leadership Network (BLN) is a national employer-led program operating in concert with the state Governors' Committees. The BLN engages the leadership and participation of companies throughout the United States to hire qualified job applicants with disabilities.

This program offers employers important disability employment information through a network of companies; the opportunity to provide training and work experience for job seekers with disabilities; and recognition for the best disability employment practices.

The Outreach to Small Business Project

The goal of the Outreach to Small Business Project is to educate small and medium-size businesses about the ADA; the benefits of hiring, retaining and promoting people with disabilities; and the resources available to these businesses.

This project utilizes the expertise of members of the employer subcommittee to develop materials and implement marketing strategies to reach small businesses, trade associations and professional service organizations.

The Cultural Diversity Initiative

The goal of the Cultural Diversity Initiative project is to improve employment opportunities for minority persons with disabilities. Recent U.S. Census Bureau statistics reveal that more than 66% of all African-Americans with disabilities are unemployed. In addition, 85% of all severely disabled African-Americans are not working. More than 59% of Hispanic persons with disabilities are unemployed. Individuals with disabilities who are members of other minority groups are also disproportionately represented among the unemployed.

In cooperation with the U.S. Department of Education's Office of Special Education and Rehabilitation Services (OSERS) and key minority organizations, a significant part of this project includes training minority individuals with disabilities, who in turn will be able to educate others within their respective communities on the ADA, disability employment issues, and how to compete for grants funded under Titles I through VIII of the Rehabilitation Act.

Another aspect of the project involves working with minority organizations to develop strategies they can pursue to reduce the high unemployment rate of minorities with disabilities.

The High School/High Tech Program

The goal of the High School/High Tech Program is to encourage students at the secondary level, and below, to take the necessary academic preparation and skill training to pursue careers in engineering, science and high technology fields. The program provides paid internships and mentoring for high school students with disabilities.

In cooperation with public and private funding sources, businesses and school districts throughout the United States, High School/High Tech programs are active in many cities across the country.

Promoting Entrepreneurial and Self-Employment Opportunities for People with Disabilities Project

The goal of this project is to identify, on a national level, appropriate resources for planning, training, technical assistance, and capital development for individuals with disabilities who wish to develop their own businesses.

Youth Leadership Forums

Youth Leadership Forums endeavor to assist states in developing youth leadership training for high school students with disabilities.

Statistical Tracking of the Employment of People with Disabilities Project

In an effort to advance the employment of people with disabilities, there must be a method by which statistics in this area are measured. Statistical tracking of the unemployment rates of people with disabilities is the only way to determine if progress is being made. The purpose of this effort, which is being coordinated with the Census Bureau and the Bureau of Labor Statistics, is to develop the country's capability to collect, prepare and distribute this type of information.

The Employment of People with Cognitive Disabilities Project

The purpose of this project is to dispel current stereotypes concerning the employability of persons with cognitive disabilities, and to develop white collar employment opportunities for these individuals, with the primary focus on people with mental retardation.

The Disabled Veterans Employment Forums

The Subcommittee on Disabled Veterans conducts regional forums to review employment issues facing veterans with disabilities in specific geographic areas. Executive summaries, identifying issues that need to be addressed, are prepared for each forum.

Perspectives on Employment of People with Disabilities in the Federal Sector

This annual conference, which is co-sponsored by 10 federal agencies and chaired by the President's Committee, brings together federal EEO officials and personnel representatives who deal with issues that affect the employment of people with disabilities within the federal government.

The Job Accommodation Network

The Job Accommodation Network (JAN) is an international toll-free consulting service that provides information about job accommodations and the employability of people with functional limitations. JAN is open to the public. Calls are handled by consultants who understand the functional limitations associated with disabilities and who have instant access to comprehensive information about accommodation methods, devices and strategies.

The mission of JAN is to assist in the hiring, retraining, retention or advancement of persons with disabilities by providing accommodation information. JAN is not an employment service, but a job accommodation service. These services are offered free.

In 1991, JAN's mission was expanded to provide public access information to businesses and services needing to comply with the ADA. For further information, the Job Accommodation Network can be reached at 1-800-526-7234 or 1-800-ADA-WORK.

CHAPTER 4:
AGE DISCRIMINATION

In General

As the baby boomer generation reaches their fifties and sixties, the American workforce is comprised of a much larger population of older employees. Many of these employees have been working for a long period of time. Thus, they are generally compensated at a much higher rate than their younger counterparts, resulting in quite an expense for the employer. This creates an economic incentive for the employer to lay off the older workers. Once unemployed, the older worker has a much more difficult time finding new employment.

In order to deal with this problem, legislation has been passed which affords some protection to older workers who face age discrimination in employment. The primary legislation enacted to combat the problem of age discrimination is the Age Discrimination in Employment Act of 1967 (ADEA), which is further discussed below.

Additional remedies may be available under state anti-discrimination laws, which may also apply in situations where the ADEA does not, e.g. in the case of private employers of less than 20 employees.

The Age Discrimination in Employment Act of 1967

Age discrimination in employment is governed by the Age Discrimination in Employment Act of 1967 (ADEA), as amended. The ADEA prohibits age discrimination in all aspects of employment, such as hiring and firing, advancement, and compensation, for persons age 40 or older. Mandatory retirement is prohibited under the ADEA except in certain limited situations. Lay-offs are particularly suspect if they only involve older workers.

Coverage

The ADEA provides protection to employees as well as job applicants. The law applies to federal, state and local employers, as well as private employers of 20 or more employees. Unions and employment agencies are also subject to the ADEA provided they meet certain criteria.

In addition to the exception for private employers of 20 or less employees, there are additional exceptions to coverage under the ADEA, as set forth below.

1. Mandatory retirement at age 65 of executives or people in high policy-making positions is permitted if the retired employee would receive annual pension benefits worth $44,000 or more.

2. Certain employees of police and fire departments, tenured university faculty, and certain federal employees engaged in enforcement and air traffic control positions, may be exempt from coverage under the ADEA.

3. If age is an essential part of one's job—i.e., it is a bona fide occupational qualification related to performance abilities—the employee may be exempt from coverage under the ADEA.

Nevertheless, as set forth above, most states have laws against age discrimination in employment which may provide protection when there is an exception under the ADEA. In fact, many of the state laws provide more comprehensive coverage than the ADEA. Therefore, the reader is advised to check the law of his or her own jurisdiction concerning protection afforded under the state anti-discrimination statutes.

Bringing an Age Discrimination Claim under the ADEA

Employees seeking to bring a claim under the ADEA must file a claim with the Equal Employment Opportunity Commission within 180 days of the discriminatory act.

Some states require that the employee first file their claim with the state's own equal employment opportunity or state human resources agency. These states are known as *deferral states*, which elect to make their own investigation prior to that of the EEOC. In deferral states, the EEOC's 180-day time limitation is extended to 300 days after the discriminatory act, or 30 days after notice that the state has terminated its proceedings.

The employee is entitled to bring a private civil suit in state or federal court against the employer 60 days after filing the complaint with the EEOC or state agency. This may be done even though the EEOC or state agency has not completed its own investigation. If, however, the EEOC files a lawsuit based on its investigation, the EEOC lawsuit preempts any action brought by the employee.

Under the statute, a lawsuit must be brought within 2 years of the discriminatory act, or 3 years if the act was willful.

In order to prevail in an age discrimination lawsuit, the employee has the burden of proving a prima facie case, which includes a showing that: (i) the employee is a member of the protected class, i.e. over 40; (ii) the employee is adversely affected by the employer's action; and (iii) age was the determining factor in the employer's action. Once a prima facie case has been demonstrated, the employer has the burden of showing that the action was taken for some legitimate nondiscriminatory reason.

If the employer is able to do so, the burden shifts again to the employee to show that the stated reason is merely a pretext. If the employee prevails, he or she may be entitled to a money damage award, and equitable relief, e.g. reinstatement.

The Federal Older Workers Benefit Protection Act of 1990

In General

Some employers attempt to lay off older workers just prior to the vesting of their pension plans. Under the Federal Older Workers Benefit Protection Act of 1990, it is illegal for an employer to: (i) use an employee's age as the basis for discrimination in benefits, and (ii) target older workers for staff cutting. Such actions would also violate the ADEA, as further discussed above.

Waivers

Employers have also been known to ask their older employees to sign waivers, i.e., agreements not to sue. The Act regulates the type of waivers that employers can ask employees to sign in connection with early retirement, and places the following restrictions on such waivers:

1. The waiver must be easily understood;

2. The waiver must specify that it covers the employees rights under the ADEA, and may not cover any rights of which the employee is unaware;

3. The employee must receive something of value in return for signing the waiver which exceeds that to which the employee is already entitled;

4. The employee must be given a certain amount of time to review the waiver before signing it; and

5. The employee must be advised that he or she has the right to consult an attorney before signing.

Further, if the offer is made to a class of employees, they must be given written information on how the class was defined, including the positions and ages of all of the class members as well as the ages of all employees in the same positions who are not being asked to sign the waiver.

CHAPTER 5:
SEXUAL HARASSMENT IN THE WORKPLACE

In General

Many women confront harassment in the workplace daily. However, it generally does not reach the level of abuse that justifies a lawsuit. Some women do not know where they can legally "draw the line." This chapter attempts to shed some light on the factors that would likely constitute harassment in a legal sense.

All individuals, male or female, are protected by laws prohibiting sexual harassment. Male employees have been known to suffer sexual harassment at the hands of other males or females. In addition, female employees have also suffered sexual harassment at the hands of other females.

However, the majority of sexual harassment complaints are brought by female employees against males. For this reason, this chapter basically focuses on female/male situations. Nevertheless, if the criteria for a sexual harassment violation is met, any individual is permitted to seek legal recourse.

Applicable Law

In 1980, the Equal Employment Opportunities Commission (EEOC) stated that sexual harassment was a form of gender discrimination which is prohibited under Title VII of the Civil Rights Act. The EEOC then issued regulations defining illegal sexual harassment. In 1986, the U.S. Supreme Court also held that sexual harassment was a form of illegal employment discrimination. In addition, most states have enacted their own laws prohibiting sexual harassment.

An individual is generally permitted to bring a claim for sexual harassment under either Title VII, or the applicable state law. Some jurisdictions may require the complainant to first file with the EEOC or the governing state agency prior to taking legal action. After the government agency completes its investigation, absent resolution of the matter, it will generally issue a "right to sue" letter which permits the complainant to proceed with litigation.

Because many state laws provide greater protection to the employee, the reader is advised to check the law in his or her own jurisdiction in this regard.

Equal Employment Opportunity Commission Standards

The standards set forth by the Equal Employment Opportunity Commission are often used as a guide for states in enacting their own sexual harassment prohibitions.

The EEOC basically defines sexual harassment as "unwelcome" sexual advances, requests for sexual favors and other verbal or physical conduct of a sexual nature when:

1. Submission to such conduct is made either explicitly or implicitly a term or condition of an individual's employment;

2. Submission to or rejection of such conduct by an individual is used as the basis for employment decisions affecting such individual; or

3. Such conduct has the purpose or effect of unreasonably interfering with an individual's work performance or creating an intimidating, hostile or offensive working environment.

Further, in 1988, the EEOC amended its guidelines to extend legal responsibility to employers for the sexual harassment of employees by nonemployees. It holds an employer responsible for the acts of nonemployees when the employer, or its agents or supervisory employees, knows or should have known of the conduct and fails to take appropriate corrective action.

Standard of Conduct

There are three major standards that are examined to determine whether behavior constitutes illegal sexual harassment, as further discussed below.

The Reasonable Female Employee Standard

The standard a court usually uses in determining whether conduct violates the law is whether or not a "reasonable" female employee would find the conduct offensive. In addition, the individual can set the boundaries of "reasonableness" for herself by communicating to the offender that she finds his behavior offensive. If he thereafter persists, he will have violated the standard of conduct she set.

Of course, to prevail in a lawsuit, there must be some proof that the communication took place, e.g. a letter to the offender and the employer, and proof that the offensive behavior persisted after the offender was notified.

The Severe and Pervasive Standard

Another factor a court uses to determine whether certain conduct consti-tutes sexual harassment is whether the behavior was so severe or pervasive that it created a hostile work environment. According to the EEOC, some factors which indicate that behavior was "severe and pervasive" include: (i) the type of behavior, e.g. whether it was verbal, physical or both; (ii) the fre-quency of the behavior; (iii) the position of the offender, e.g., supervisor or co-worker; (iv) the number of individuals who engaged in such behaviors; and (v) whether the behavior was directed at one or more individuals.

Of course, certain types of behavior do not have to be cumulative, but need only occur once to be deemed illegal, e.g. employment or promotions that are conditioned on sexual favors, or outright sexual attacks.

The Unwelcome Conduct Standard

Although it may appear that any behavior which gives rise to a complaint would qualify as "unwelcome," the court may examine additional criteria to make its determination, such as whether the behavior was unwelcome at the time it occurred.

For example, a female employee may have engaged in sexual behavior with another voluntarily at one time. However, if thereafter she has commu-nicated her desire not to continue in such a relationship, any subsequent sex-ual demands placed upon her would be deemed "unwelcome" and would likely constitute illegal sexual harassment.

In addition, even if the woman "voluntarily" goes along with the offen-sive behavior, if she does so out of fear of losing her job, this would also con-stitute "unwelcome" behavior.

Examples of Sexual Harassment in the Workplace

The following conduct would likely constitute unlawful sexual harass-ment in the workplace:

Sexual Advances

Supervisors

Concerning the attempt to gain sexual favors from an employee, the con-duct of an authority figure will be scrutinized more closely because of the power he or she may have over the employee, such as promotions, etc. It is the perceived threat of requiring sexual favors as the basis for making employment-related decisions that determines whether the conduct constitutes sexual harassment. In addition, there is a presumption that the employer has knowledge, or should have knowledge, of the illegal behavior.

Co-Workers

If the sexual advances are made by a co-worker, the determination is less clearcut because the co-worker does not have any "power" over the female employee. Instead, the court will look more at the nature of the behavior, e.g., the language and/or gestures used, the frequency and persistency of the advances, etc.

In addition, the presumption of employer knowledge is not applicable when the offender is a co-worker. The female employee generally must put the co-worker and the employee "on notice" that the conduct is unwelcome and will not be tolerated.

The Sexually Offensive Atmosphere

Courts have recognized that creating a sexually offensive atmosphere—e.g., by displaying pornographic materials in the workplace, or by engaging in vulgar and lewd behavior—is a violation of sexual harassment laws. This is so even if the offensive conduct is not directed at any particular individual.

The concern is that the creation of such a sexually offensive atmosphere demeans, and works to the disadvantage of, the female employees. It is difficult for a female employee to be taken seriously when surrounded by lewd and humiliating representations of women.

If anticipating bringing this type of claim, one should try and confiscate the offensive pictures or documents as evidence. In addition, a journal should be kept with entries detailing offensive remarks, jokes, etc., including the date, time, place and individuals present.

The Hostile Work Environment

Creation of a hostile work environment usually involves intimidation tactics used to try and force women out of a traditionally all-male industry. Even if there is no sexual misconduct, the courts have still found there to be a sexual harassment violation. The courts will look at whether the offensive behavior would have been directed at a male employee.

This type of hostile conduct may also form the basis of a sexual discrimination case. In fact, the laws prohibiting sexual harassment were, in large part, based upon sexual discrimination statutes.

CHAPTER 6:
THE EMPLOYEE'S RIGHT TO FAIR PAY

The Fair Labor Standards Act

An employee's right to receive fair pay and other related matters is governed by the Fair Labor Standards Act (FLSA). The FLSA sets forth the applicable federal minimum wage and overtime requirements, and regulates child labor.

Historical Background

The Fair Labor Standards Act was enacted in 1938 by President Roosevelt following the Great Depression, in order to place controls over employers who were paying unfair wages under insufferable working conditions, and engaging in onerous child labor.

At the time it was enacted, the Act only applied to industries whose combined employment represented about one-fifth of the labor force. The Act set the minimum hourly wage at 25 cents, and the maximum workweek at 44 hours.

In 1940, to avoid economic disaster in Puerto Rico and the Virgin Islands caused by the minimum wage requirement upon their industries, a special exception was made. An amendment was enacted which established special industry committees to determine the minimum wage levels applicable in Puerto Rico and the Virgin Islands. These levels were permitted to be less than the statutory rates applicable elsewhere in the United States.

Subsequent amendments to the FLSA extended the law's coverage to additional employees and raised the level of the minimum wage. In 1949, the minimum wage was raised from 40 cents an hour to 75 cents an hour for all workers. Coverage was extended to employees in the air transport industry. A 1955 amendment increased the minimum wage to $1.00 an hour with no changes in coverage.

The 1961 amendments greatly expanded the FLSA's scope in the retail trade sector and increased the minimum for previously covered workers to $1.15 an hour effective September 1961 and to $1.25 an hour in September 1963. The minimum for newly covered workers was set at $1.00 an hour effective September 1961; $1.15 an hour in September 1964; and $1.25 an hour in September 1965.

Retail and service establishments were permitted to employ full-time students at wages of no more than 15 percent below the minimum with proper certification from the Department of Labor. The amendments extended coverage to employees of retail trade enterprises with sales exceeding $1 million annually, although individual establishments within those covered enterprises were exempt if their annual sales fell below $250,000. These amendments extended coverage in the retail trade industry from an established 250,000 workers to 2.2 million.

In 1966, the enterprise sales volume test was lowered to $500,000 effective February 1967, thus further broadening coverage. The amendments also extended coverage to public schools, nursing homes, laundries, and the entire construction industry. In addition, farms were subject to coverage for the first time if their employment reached a specified labor force. The 1966 amendments also extended the full-time student certification program to covered agricultural employers and to institutions of higher learning.

In February 1967, the minimum wage was raised to $1.00 per hour for newly covered non-farm workers, with additional raises scheduled at $1.15 in February 1968, $1.30 in February 1969, $1.45 in February 1970, and $1.60 in February 1971.

In 1974, coverage was extended to all nonsupervisory employees of Federal, State, and local governments and many domestic workers. However, a subsequent Supreme Court ruling exempted State and local government workers engaged in traditional government functions.

The minimum wage increased to $2.00 an hour in 1974, $2.10 in 1975, and $2.30 in 1976 for all except farm workers, whose minimum initially rose to $1.60. Parity with nonfarm workers was reached at $2.30 with the 1977 amendments.

The 1977 amendments eliminated the separate lower minimum wage for agricultural workers and set a new uniform wage schedule for all covered workers. The minimum went to $2.65 an hour in January 1978, $2.90 in January 1979, $3.10 in January 1980, and $3.35 in January 1981.

In addition, these amendments permitted the employment of younger children to work in the agricultural industry, and relaxed the provisions for businesses who were permitted to employ students at a lower wage rate. Further, the overtime exemption for employees in hotels, motels, and restaurants was eliminated.

To allow for the effects of inflation, the $250,000 dollar volume of sales coverage test for retail trade and service enterprises was increased in stages to $362,500 after December 31, 1981.

In 1985, as a result of a Supreme Court ruling, an amendment to the Act was enacted which permitted State and local governments to compensate their employees for overtime hours with compensatory time-off instead of overtime pay, at a rate of 1-1/2 hours for each hour of overtime worked.

In 1989, a single annual dollar volume test of $500,000 for enterprise coverage of both retail and non-retail businesses was established. In addition, the minimum wage and overtime pay exemption for small retail firms was eliminated. Therefore, employees of small retail businesses became covered by the minimum wage and overtime pay provisions of the Act in any workweek in which they engaged in interstate commerce, or the production of goods for commerce.

In addition, the minimum wage was raised to $3.80 an hour beginning April 1, 1990, and to $4.25 an hour beginning April 1, 1991. A special training wage provision rate of 85% of the minimum wage, but not less than $3.35 an hour, was established for employees under the age of twenty. However, this provision expired in 1993.

These amendments also established civil money penalties against employers who willfully or repeatedly violate the minimum wage or overtime pay provisions of the law.

The FLSA was again amended in 1996. The basic provisions of the existing law, as amended are set forth below.

Basic Provisions

The Federal Minimum Wage

Under the Fair Labor Standards Act, an employee has certain rights concerning wages. Almost 10 million American workers are paid minimum wage rates. Although the minimum wage was historically sufficient to maintain an adequate standard of living, inflation recently brought the prevailing minimum wage to a 40 year low.

In an effort to raise the standard of living for minimum wage workers, the federal minimum wage was raised to $5.15 per hour effective September 1, 1997. The reader is advised to also check his or her state's minimum wage laws, because federal minimum wage laws defer to the state's minimum wage law, provided the state sets a higher rate than the federal government.

Overtime Pay

Overtime pay must be at least one and one-half times the employee's regular rate of pay for all hours worked over 40 in a workweek. Some employers will give their employees extra time off from work instead of paying overtime wages. This is known as *compensatory time* because it "compensates" the employee for the extra hours worked.

However, unless the employer is a state or government agency, the substitution of compensatory time for premium pay is generally unlawful. In those situations where compensatory time is legal, the employer must grant the employee leave time which is one and one-half times the hours worked.

For example, if an employee works 50 hours in a regular 40 hour week, he or she is entitled to 15 hours of compensatory time, i.e., the 10 additional hours worked multiplied by one and one-half.

Compensatory time is also subject to a mutual agreement between the employer and employee, or pursuant to an agreement made by union representatives on behalf of the employees. Additional rules may apply when compensatory time is permitted in the private sector, therefore, the reader is advised to check the law of his or her jurisdiction.

Child Labor

An employee must be at least 16 years old to work in most non-farm jobs and at least 18 to work in non-farm jobs declared hazardous by the Secretary of Labor. Children aged 14 and 15 are permitted to work outside school hours in various non-manufacturing, non-mining, non-hazardous jobs provided they work no more than 3 hours on a school day or 18 hours in a school week; and 8 hours on a non-school day or 40 hours in a non-school week.

In addition, work may not begin before 7 a.m. or end after 7 p.m., excluding June 1st through Labor Day, when evening hours may be extended to 9 p.m. Different rules apply in agricultural employment.

Violations of the child labor provisions of the law can result in fines of up to $10,000 per child.

Commuting Time

The manner in which employers treat commuting time by employees who travel in an employer's vehicle was changed. Time spent in travel by an employee in an employer-provided vehicle, or in activities performed by an employee which are incidental to the use of the vehicle, are not deemed "hours worked" and, therefore, do not have to be paid.

However, this provision only applies if the travel is within the normal commuting area for the employer's business; and the use of the vehicle is subject to an agreement between the employer and the employee or the employee's representative.

Computer Professionals

There was a change in the provisions under which some professional employees in the computer field qualify for exemption from the minimum wage and overtime pay requirements. The exemption from overtime pay for certain computer professionals now exempts these workers if they are paid at least $27.63 an hour.

Tips

Many employees in service industries, such as hair stylists and waitresses, receive tips from their customers in addition to their wages. However, employers are generally permitted to offset a portion of those tips against the minimum wage requirement, although the employee's salary cannot fall below the legal minimum wage.

Basically, an employer may credit a certain amount of the tips against its minimum wage obligation when certain conditions are met. The law now sets the employer's cash wage obligation at not less than $2.13 an hour. This replaces the former provision requiring that tipped employees be paid at least 50 percent of the minimum wage in cash.

However, if an employee's tips combined with the employer's cash wage of $2.13 an hour do not equal the minimum hourly wage, the employer must make up the difference.

The Opportunity Wage Provision

The law sets forth an "Opportunity Wage" of $4.25 per hour, which is a below-minimum rate that employers can pay employees who are under 20 years of age during their first 90 days of employment.

Special Certificates

The law also provides that certain full-time students, student learners, apprentices, and workers with disabilities may be paid less than the minimum wage under special certificates issued by the Department of Labor.

On-Call Employees

Some employees are asked to be "on call" on their days off. If during this time the employee is prevented from enjoying or benefitting from the time off because of certain requirements of the employer, e.g., the employee cannot travel beyond reach, it is generally compensable. However, if the employee is free to use this time as they see fit, it is generally not compensable except for the time that they are actually called in to work.

Paid Vacations

Employees have no legal right to paid vacations. It is entirely up to an employer whether they want to provide their employees with this benefit. In addition, an employer can place certain constraints on providing an employee with any vacation time whatsoever.

Covered Employers

The FLSA applies to all federal, state or local government agencies. In addition, employers who engage in interstate commerce, or whose annual sales total $500,000 or more, are also covered under the FLSA.

Because most employers are deemed to have engaged in interstate commerce, i.e., business which crosses state lines, there is a relatively small number of employers who are not covered. The FLSA also generally applies to domestic workers, such as nannies and housekeepers.

Covered employers are required to abide by the FLSA unless a state or other federal law requires a higher standard. For this reason, the reader is advised to check the law of his or her jurisdiction to ascertain whether an applicable state law provides greater employee protection.

Exemptions

The FLSA also sets forth a number of exemptions. Some of these exempt employers include small local farms; farmworkers; certain professional, executive, and administrative employees; certain fishermen; newspersons who are employed by local newspapers with a maximum circulation of

4000; employees who work outside of the United States and its territories; and certain other specified categories of workers. Independent contractors are also not covered under the FLSA as they are not deemed to be employees.

The Wage and Hour Division of the Employment Standards Administration

The FLSA is administered by the Department of Labor through the Wage and Hour Division of the Employment Standards Administration. Their objective is to achieve compliance with labor standards through enforcement, and administrative, and educational programs.

The Wage and Hour Division was created with the enactment of the Fair Labor Standards Act in 1938. It is responsible for the administration and enforcement of a wide range of employment-related laws, and employs a nationwide staff of investigators, supervisors, and technical and clerical workers.

The Wage and Hour Division enforces the Federal minimum wage, overtime pay, recordkeeping, and the child labor requirements of the Fair Labor Standards Act. They also enforce a number of other laws, including the Employee Polygraph Protection Act; the Family and Medical Leave Act, the wage garnishment provisions of the Consumer Credit Protection Act; the "whistleblower" provisions of several environmental impact laws; the Migrant and Seasonal Agricultural Worker Protection Act; the prevailing wage requirements of the Davis Bacon Act and the Service Contract Act; and other statutes applicable to Federal contracts for construction and for the provision of goods and services.

In an effort to assist employers in complying with the law, The Wage and Hour Division provides information to employers, employees, labor unions, community groups, and trade associations.

Investigation and Enforcement

The Wage and Hour Division employs investigators who inquire into employee complaints of minimum wage violations by their employers. In addition, certain trades known to abuse the minimum wage law, such as the garment industry, are often subjected to investigations whether or not an employee complaint is made.

This is so because many of the workers commonly employed in these businesses are not organized, do not speak the language, are not knowledgeable about the law, and fear retaliation. Thus, they are less likely to make their complaints known.

There are stiff civil and criminal penalties available for employers who do not abide by the law. Fines of up to $10,000 per violation may be assessed against employers who violate the child labor provisions of the law and up to $1,000 per violation against employers who willfully or repeatedly violate the minimum wage or overtime pay provisions.

In addition, the Department of Labor may recover back wages for employees who have been underpaid in violation of the law, and those employers found to be in violation may face civil or criminal action against them.

The law also prohibits an employer from taking any adverse action—e.g. discharge or demotion—against any employee who files a complaint or participates in any proceedings under the Act.

A Directory of District Offices for the Wage and Hour Division of the Employment Standards Administration is set forth in the Appendix.

Payroll Deductions

There are certain deductions an employer is legally required to take from an employee's salary, as further set forth below.

Taxes

Employers are required to withhold taxes from their employees' salaries, make periodic deposits, and file quarterly payroll tax returns. Employers are responsible for the following withholding taxes:

Federal Income Tax

Federal income tax is money withheld from an employee's earnings based on gross income, number of dependents, marital status, etc.

State Income Tax

Approximately 41 states require the employer to withhold state income tax.

State Unemployment Insurance Tax

State Unemployment Insurance Tax is determined and controlled by the employer based on its own unemployment experience.

State Disability Insurance

State disability insurance is also assessed on employees by some states, and is determined by setting a maximum withholding amount and/or a wage base.

Social Security

Social Security is paid by both the employer and employee. The employer is responsible for collection and payment of the employee's contribution.

The Equal Pay Act of 1963

The Equal Pay Act, an amendment to the Fair Labor Standards Act, provides that equal pay must be paid workers for equal work, regardless of gender, if the jobs they perform require "equal skill, effort, and responsibility and are performed under similar working conditions." Most private employers are subject to this act, which covers both current employees and job applicants.

Although discrimination in pay based on sex is also prohibited by Title VII of the Civil Rights Act, the Equal Pay Act serves to cover employers who may not be subject to Title VII due to the size of the company.

Employee Records

In order to take full advantage of the protections afforded under the law, it is important for the employee to understand his or her rights, and take the initiative to make sure he or she is fairly compensated. It is crucial that the employee keep an independent record of hours worked. Employers have been known to make numerous mistakes in calculating paychecks.

Thus, one should not assume that the employer is always right. It is important to cross-check all of the entries on the paystub against one's own records. If an item is contradictory or confusing, don't hesitate to bring it to the attention of the payroll department for explanation and correction.

CHAPTER 7:
THE EMPLOYEE'S RIGHT TO PRIVACY
IN THE WORKPLACE

In General

Every American is entitled to maintain a certain degree of privacy concerning their personal affairs. One does not expect a stranger to open and read their personal mail, or eavesdrop on telephone calls placed from home. This chapter discusses the extent to which an employee's privacy rights are protected while they are on their job, and the legal remedies available when those rights are violated.

Computers

The advent of computer technology was accompanied by a number of concerns over privacy rights in the workplace, as set forth below.

Electronic Mail

Much of today's communication takes place through the use of a computer. For example, many workers have access to a computer through which they can send electronic messages —commonly referred to as "E-mail"—to another computer user.

Whether or not an employee can expect privacy of their E-mail depends largely on what type of system the employer utilizes. For example, E-mail sent on a public access system would not likely be intercepted by one's employer. However, an employer would probably be able to access E-mail which takes place within the company's internal system, and they often do. Thus, an employee would not be well advised to put offensive material on their E-mail because they could risk dismissal.

Private Files

Employees often use their computers at work to create private files. Employees generally have a right to expect that personal files are private. This is particularly so if the employee maintains a password necessary for accessing these files. An employer who accesses an employee's private files must generally demonstrate that there was a valid business purpose for doing so.

Telephone Privacy

Employers are generally entitled to monitor business-related telephone calls which are placed to or from the business. Such monitoring is often undertaken, e.g. so that the quality of service rendered by employees in customer service positions can be monitored.

The Electronic Communications Privacy Act

The Electronic Communications Privacy Act (ECPA) which was originally enacted to regulate wiretapping, also put restrictions on the employer's right to monitor employee phone calls, as set forth below. For example, if a telephone line is being monitored for business reasons, and a personal call comes through to an employee, the employer must disconnect.

However, if the employee has consented to the monitoring of personal calls, the employer does not have to disconnect. Some states require that consent must be given by both the employee and the other party to the call in order to permit monitoring by the employer.

Voice Mail

Voice mail messaging has become commonplace. It appears that the ECPA also provides some protection to employees who have voice mail systems. The ECPA provides that an employer may be held liable if it obtains, reads, discloses, deletes or prevents access to an employee's voice mail messages that are in electronic storage.

The Employee Polygraph Protection Act

In making a decision to hire, many employers would like the right to conduct a lie detector test of every prospective employee. In addition, employers would also like to be able to force existing employees to submit to a lie detector test if the need arises, e.g. where there is suspicion of internal theft. However, under the Employee Polygraph Protection Act, most private employers are prohibited from using lie detector tests in either situation.

Nevertheless, there are certain exemptions to the Act. For example, the federal, state, and local governments are not subject to the law. In addition, private employers who are engaged in the manufacture, distribution, or dispensing of pharmaceuticals; and security services, such as security guard services, are permitted to administer lie detector tests to certain prospective employees, subject to restrictions.

There are also situations in which the Act permits testing of persons suspected of employee theft that resulted in economic loss to the employer, also subject to restrictions.

In those situations where lie detector tests are legally permitted, the employee has certain rights relating to the length and conduct of the test. In addition, the employer is required to give the employee advance written notice. An employee may refuse to take the test or may request to discontinue taking the test during its administration. The results of an employee's lie detector test are private and are not permitted to be disclosed to any unauthorized person.

Violations of the Act may result in civil penalties up to $10,000. Legal action may be brought by a job applicant, an employee, or by the Secretary of Labor. In addition, where a specific state law or collective bargaining agreement provides for a more restrictive ban on lie detector tests, the federal government defers to that law.

CHAPTER 8:
HEALTH AND SAFETY IN THE WORKPLACE

In General

Over the past 20 years, there has been a concerted effort by America's workers to have effective legislation passed which would protect their health and safety in the workplace. Through this effort, they have been successful in getting some major legislation enacted which addresses health and safety concerns on the job. A number of laws now establish basic safety standards which have as their goal a reduction in the number of workplace deaths, injuries and illnesses.

All businesses are now required by law to provide a safe and healthy workplace for their employees. To make sure they are in compliance, an employer may engage the services of a workplace safety consultant, who specializes in bringing companies into compliance with the law.

Some safety initiatives the employer can take include: (i) regular in-house safety inspections; (ii) a comprehensive safety plan for all employees; and (iii) the maintenance of adequate protective clothing and equipment where the nature of business operations requires such precautions. There should also be an adequately stocked first-aid kit readily available, and the telephone numbers for emergency medical assistance should be on display for quick reference if the needs arises.

Statutory requirements may vary from state to state. Therefore, it is essential that the reader investigate the particular requirements of his or her jurisdiction, as well as the federal regulations promoting health and safety in the workplace, as more fully described below.

The Occupational Safety and Health Act

The Occupational Safety and Health Act of 1970, provides job safety and health protection for workers by promoting safe and healthful working conditions throughout the nation. The Act is administered by the Occupational Safety and Health Administration (OSHA), a division of the U.S. Department of Labor. OSHA protects just about every working individual with the exception of miners, transportation workers, certain public employees and self-employed persons.

OSHA and its state governmental partners utilize a combined staff which includes inspectors, complaint discrimination investigators, engineers, physicians, educators, standards writers, and other technical and support personnel. The OSHA staff establishes and enforces protective standards to be used in the workplace, and sponsors workplace safety and health programs for employers and employees.

Under the Act, employers are required to maintain their facilities free from any recognized hazards that are causing, or are likely to cause, death or serious harm to an employee. The employees are also required to comply with all applicable sections of the occupational safety and health standards issued by OSHA.

A directory of regional OSHA offices is set forth in the Appendix.

Whistle Blowers

If a workplace situation exists that appears to be unsafe or unhealthy, a complaint requesting an inspection may be filed with the nearest OSHA office. Most workplace safety laws, to be effective, rely on employees to report employment hazards. These employees are generally known as "whistle blowers."

To prevent retaliation and encourage compliance, it is illegal for employers to fire or otherwise discriminate against employees who report unsafe conditions to proper authorities. If an employee who "blew the whistle" believes that they have suffered discrimination as a result, the employee can file a complaint with OSHA within 30 days of the alleged incident.

Making an OSHA Complaint

In order to prevail on a complaint brought under OSHA, the employee must generally prove that (i) the employer failed to keep the workplace free of a hazard; and (ii) the particular hazard was recognized as being likely to cause death or serious physical injury.

Before bringing a formal legal action, an employee concerned about workplace hazards should first discuss the matter with his or her employer. If the employer fails to remedy the problem, a complaint can be filed with OSHA.

Citations

If OSHA determines, after an inspection, that an employer is in violation of the law, it issues a citation against that employer. The citation specifies each and every violation alleged to have been committed by the employer and the date by which the violation must be corrected. The employer is required to display the citation at or near the location of the violation for a period of three days or until the violation is corrected, whichever date is later. The purpose of this provision is to warn the employees about the dangerous condition.

Penalties for Noncompliance

The penalties for failure to adhere to the Act are serious. For example, there are mandatory civil penalties of up to $7,000 per violation against employers for serious violations of the law, and optional penalties of up to $7,000 for nonserious violations. If an employer fails to correct a violation within the allotted time period, additional penalties of up to $7,000 per day can be assessed until the violation is finally corrected.

Willful violations of the Act can result in penalties ranging from a minimum of $5,000 to a maximum of $70,000. Repeated violations can also result in a fine of up to $70,000. An employer can also be assessed a penalty of up to $7,000 for failure to display the citation as required.

In addition to the civil penalties, criminal penalties may be assessed if a willful violation of the Act results in the death of an employee. Upon conviction, such a violation is punishable by a fine of up to $250,000 or by imprisonment of up to six months, or both. If the employer is a corporation, the maximum fine is $500,000. There are additional penalties that may be imposed for subsequent convictions.

OSHA offers free assistance to employers in identifying and correcting workplace safety and health hazards. Employers requesting such assistance are not subject to citation or penalty. OSHA has a 24 hour hotline available for reporting workplace safety and health emergencies (1-800-321-OSHA).

Recordkeeping

Under the Act, employers are required to report to OSHA concerning their compliance with the various prescribed standards of safety and health. Although the required OSHA reports are relatively simple, they are quite important. The documents include a summary and log of occupational injuries and illnesses, which must be filed annually, and a supplemental report describing each incident in detail.

Smoking in the Workplace

It has been clearly established that tobacco smoke is detrimental to one's health. This health hazard also applies to secondhand smoke one inhales when in the company of smokers. In fact, according to the Environmental Protection Agency, secondhand tobacco smoke kills about 3,700 Americans per year. To protect nonsmokers from smokers, many employers either restrict smoking to designated areas, or prohibit it altogether.

Presently, there are no federal laws which prohibit smoking in the workplace. Many states and local governments, however, have enacted legislation restricting smoking on the job. On the other hand, many states have laws which prohibit discrimination against smokers who smoke during nonworking hours. Thus, the reader is advised to check the law of his or her jurisdiction.

Workers' Compensation

When an employee suffers a work-related injury or illness, and as a result becomes disabled and unable to work, he or she may be entitled to receive certain benefits under a system known as workers' compensation. The Federal government and every state administers some type of workers' compensation program according to its own statutory scheme.

Because statutory provisions vary depending on the particular jurisdiction, the reader is advised to check the law of his or her own jurisdiction concerning specific questions.

Workers' compensation laws came into being in the early 20th century to try and address the growing problem of work-related injuries and illnesses which accompanied the era of Industrial Revolution. Before workers' compensation laws were enacted, a disabled worker's only recourse was to prevail in a lawsuit against his or her employer, a costly and time-consuming process. Workers' compensation statutes provided a trade-off. The statutes basically eliminate fault and focus on treating and compensating the injured employee. In return for maintaining workers' compensation insurance, the employer is granted immunity from civil lawsuit.

Presently, the Federal Government, all 50 states, Puerto Rico, the U.S. Virgin Islands, American Samoa and Guam, have workers' compensation laws. Most workers are covered by their own state's workers' compensation program unless they fall under those categories entitled to Federal coverage. Federal statutes have been enacted to provide coverage for certain classes of employees.

In the majority of states, workers' compensation coverage is mandatory. Employers who fail to maintain the required insurance may be sued by the employee, and are liable for damages. Depending on the jurisdiction, non-complying employers may be further penalized.

In a minority of jurisdictions, workers' compensation coverage is elective, i.e., the employer may choose to reject the workers' compensation system. However, if a suit for damages is brought by an injured employee, the employer cannot assert the three common law defenses of contributory negligence, assumption of risk, or fellow servant negligence doctrines.

Workers' compensation claims generally fall into three categories: (i) Injury Claims; (ii) Occupational Disease Claims; and (iii) Death Claims. The injury or accident claim is the most common type of workers' compensation claim. It is generally called a "traumatic" injury claim in that it is a sudden and unexpected occurrence caused by a particular event. The occupational disease claim applies when the employee suffers a work-related illness.

Under certain circumstances, an employee may not be covered under workers' compensation. For example, injuries or illnesses which are caused by an employee's intoxication—e.g., by drugs or alcohol—are not eligible for compensation. Coverage may also be denied in situations involving:

Self-inflicted injuries, or injuries sustained while attempting to injure another;

Injuries sustained while committing a crime;

Injuries sustained when the employee was not on the job; and

Injuries sustained when the employee's conduct violated company policy.

Although the employer is generally immune from liability under workers' compensation law, the employee maintains his or her right to sue any negligent third parties who may have caused or contributed to a workplace injury, such as the manufacturer of defective machinery.

A more detailed discussion of state and federal Workers' Compensation programs can be found in this author's book entitled *Workers' Compensation Law*, also published by Oceana Publishing Company.

CHAPTER 9:
INDEPENDENT CONTRACTORS

In General

An independent contractor is generally defined as a person who contracts with another to perform services for that person, but who is not controlled by the other nor subject to the other's right to control with respect to the performance.

Whether a worker is deemed an employee or an independent contractor is important to both the worker and the employer. An employer-employee relationship is very different from the relationship between an employer who hires an independent contractor. Employees have a special legal status. Employers have certain responsibilities towards employees that they do not have when they engage the services of an independent contractor.

Because an independent contractor is not an employee, the business owner does not have to withhold tax from his or her check, nor does the employer have to contribute to Social Security or unemployment tax on behalf of the independent contractor.

In addition, the tax treatment of an employee is very different from that of an independent contractor. For this reason, the Internal Revenue Service may attempt to reclassify independent contractors as employees. This can be very costly to the employer, in that the employer would then be liable for withholding tax, Social Security contributions, and unemployment tax withholding, as well as penalties and interest on those amounts due.

Advantages vs. Disadvantages

There are advantages and disadvantages to being an independent contractor, as set forth below.

Advantages

1. The independent contractor receives a gross income check with no deductions for taxes, social security or other customary deductions from an employee's paycheck. Instead, the independent contractor estimates his or her taxes and pays those estimated amounts to the IRS at certain yearly intervals.

2. Independent contractors make a higher salary on average over employees. This is primarily due to the fact that the employer does not have to pay benefits and taxes on behalf of the independent contractor.

3. An independent contractor is entitled to certain tax deductions that an employee does not have. For example, business expenses are deductible, such as equipment, space rental, utilities, transportation, entertainment, etc.

4. There is a certain amount of freedom in that an independent contractor makes all his or her own business decisions, including what jobs to take, how much to charge, when to work, etc.

Disadvantages

1. There is no job security because the independent contractor is only paid until the job he or she was hired for is completed. There is no guarantee of a weekly paycheck. Of course, employees are also subject to dismissal or lay-offs.

2. An independent contractor is not entitled to any benefits from the hiring company. For example, an independent contractor is responsible for obtaining his or her own health insurance.

3. An independent contractor is not entitled to unemployment or workers' compensation benefits.

4. An independent contractor must pay self-employment taxes, which includes their Social Security and Medicare taxes.

Determining Status

To determine whether or not an individual is likely to be reclassified by the IRS from independent contractor status to employee status, courts have established 20 common law factors which must be taken into account. The factors that may indicate employee status are the following:

1. If the worker is required to comply with the employer's instruction as to when, where, and how he is to work.

2. If the employer trains the worker to perform in a particular manner.

3. If the employer requires the worker to render personal service.

4. If the employer hires, supervises, and pays the worker's staff.

5. If the employer and the worker have a continuing relationship.

6. If the worker is required to work during hours set by the employer.

7. If the worker is required to work full-time for the employer.

8. If the worker performs the work on the employer's premises, particularly if the work could be performed elsewhere.

9. If the employer requires the worker to perform services in a particular order or sequence.

10. If the worker is required to submit oral or written reports to the employer.

11. If payment is made by the hour, week, or month as opposed to a per job basis.

12. If the employer pays the worker's business or traveling expenses.

13. If the employer furnishes the tools and materials to the worker.

14. If there is a lack of investment by the worker in the facilities required to perform services and dependence on the employer for such facilities.

15. If the worker realizes no profit or loss as a result of the services rendered.

16. If the worker works exclusively for the employer.

17. If the worker does not make his or her services available to the general public.

18. If the employer maintains the right to discharge the worker, which would not be possible if the individual were an independent contractor working under a contract.

19. If the worker has the right to end the relationship with the employer without continuing to render services. An independent contractor would be bound by the contract to finish the job.

20. If the worker's services are integral to the business operations.

In addition to the above criteria, Section 530 of the Revenue Act of 1978 serves as a "safe harbor" for employers who treated individuals as independent contractors for federal employment tax purposes, even if they were in error, as long as the employer had a reasonable basis for doing so.

CHAPTER 10:
THE FAMILY AND MEDICAL LEAVE ACT

In General

The federally mandated Family and Medical Leave Act (FMLA) became effective in August 1993. The FMLA provides that eligible employees have the right to 12 weeks of unpaid leave in certain situations. Further, upon returning to work, the employee is entitled to be placed in the same or an equivalent job, i.e., one with the same rate of pay, benefits, and conditions of employment, including duties and responsibilities substantially similar to the previous position.

While the FMLA and similar state laws provide a start, the solution to family leave problems will not likely come from legislation. Some employers, mindful of the gap between legal rights to leave and reality help employees juggle work and family responsibilities in various ways, including allowing employees to work part of the time out of their home, or permitting flexible work hours.

Covered Employers

The FMLA applies to all public agencies, including state, local and federal employers, local schools, and private-sector employers who employed 50 or more employees in 20 or more workweeks in the current or preceding calendar year and who are engaged in commerce or in any industry or activity affecting commerce— including joint employers and successors of covered employers.

Covered employers must post a notice approved by the Secretary of Labor explaining an employee's rights and responsibilities under the FMLA. An employer that willfully violates this posting requirement may be fined up to $100 for each separate offense.

Also, covered employers must inform employees of their rights and responsibilities under the FMLA, including giving specific written information on what is required of the employee and what might happen in certain circumstances, such as if the employee fails to return to work after FMLA leave expires.

Eligibility

To be eligible for FMLA benefits, an employee must:

(1) work for a covered employer;

(2) have worked for the employer for a total of 12 months;

(3) have worked at least 1,250 hours over the previous 12 months; and

(4) work at a location in the United States or in any territory or possession of the United States where at least 50 employees are employed by the employer.

Employees seeking to use FMLA leave are required to provide 30-day advance notice of the need to take FMLA leave when the need is foreseeable and such notice is practicable.

Employers may also require employees to provide (i) medical certification supporting the need for leave due to a serious health condition affecting the employee or an immediate family member; (ii) second or third medical opinions paid for by the employer, and periodic recertification; and (iii) periodic reports during FMLA leave regarding the employee's status and intent to return to work.

For purposes of the FMLA, the "immediate family" includes the employee's spouse, children, and parents. The term "parent" does not include a parent "in-law." Children age 18 or over are not included unless they are "incapable of self-care" because of a mental or physical disability that limits one or more of the "major life activities" as those terms are defined in regulations issued by the EEOC under the ADA.

An "eligible" employee who has met FMLA's notice and certification requirements may not be denied FMLA leave provided he or she has not used up their maximum leave time for that year.

Further, it is unlawful for any employer to interfere with or restrain or deny the exercise of any right provided under this law. Employers cannot use the taking of FMLA leave as a negative factor in employment actions, such as hiring, promotions or disciplinary actions.

Benefits

The FMLA provides certain employees with up to 12 weeks of unpaid, job-protected leave a year, and requires the employee's group health benefits to be maintained during the leave. Other benefits, including cash payments chosen by the employee instead of group health insurance coverage, need not be maintained during periods of unpaid FMLA leave.

Certain types of earned benefits, such as seniority or paid leave, need not continue to accrue during periods of unpaid FMLA leave provided that such benefits do not accrue for employees who go out on other types of unpaid leave. For other benefits, such as elected life insurance coverage, the employer and the employee may make arrangements to continue benefits during periods of unpaid FMLA leave.

Leave Time

The leave permitted under the FMLA does not have to be taken all at once. Under some circumstances, employees may take FMLA leave intermittently — which means taking leave in blocks of time, or by reducing their normal weekly or daily work schedule. FMLA leave may be taken intermittently whenever medically necessary to care for a seriously ill family member, or because the employee is seriously ill and unable to work.

If FMLA leave is for birth and care or placement for adoption or foster care, use of intermittent leave is subject to the employer's approval. For example, it can be used to shorten the work week for the employee who does not want to work full time following the birth of a child.

Although companies are not required to pay employees who take leave, they may require or allow employees to apply any available vacation time and sick leave to the 12 weeks permitted under the FMLA.

Many businesses are concerned that employees who simply want to take an unpaid vacation will claim to be seriously ill to qualify for FMLA covered leave. To address that concern, the FMLA has defined "serious illness" as one which requires at least one overnight stay in a hospital or continuing treatment by or under the supervision of a health care worker. Although not required, there are official FMLA medical certification forms available through the U.S. Department of Labor Wage and Hour Division.

Spouses employed by the same employer are jointly entitled to a combined total of 12 weeks of family leave for the birth and care of a newborn child, for placement of a child for adoption or foster care, and to care for a parent who has a serious health condition. Leave for birth and care, or placement for adoption or foster care must conclude within 12 months of the birth or placement.

FMLA leave and workers' compensation leave can run together, provided the reason for the absence is due to a qualifying serious illness or injury and the employer properly notifies the employee in writing that the leave will be counted as FMLA leave.

The employer may only inquire of the employee concerning his or her use of FMLA leave. The employer is permitted to ask the employee questions to confirm whether the leave qualifies for FMLA purposes, and may require periodic reports on the employee's status and intent to return to work.

Nevertheless, the employer may have a health care provider representing the employer contact the employee's health care provider, with the employee's permission, to clarify information in the medical certification or to confirm that it was provided by the health care provider. However, the inquiry may not seek additional information regarding the health condition of the employee or his or her family member.

Return to Employment

In General

Upon return from FMLA leave, an employee must be restored to the employee's original job, or to an equivalent job with equivalent pay, benefits, and other terms and conditions of employment. In addition, an employee's use of FMLA leave cannot result in the loss of any employment benefit that the employee earned or was entitled to before using FMLA leave.

Key Employees

A "key" employee is a salaried "eligible" employee who is among the highest paid ten percent of employees within 75 miles of the work site.

Under specified and limited circumstances where restoration to employment will cause substantial and grievous economic injury to its operations, an employer may refuse to reinstate"key" employees after using FMLA leave during which health coverage was maintained. In order to do so, the employer must:

1. Notify the employee of his/her status as a "key" employee in response to the employee's notice of intent to take FMLA leave;

2. Notify the employee as soon as the employer decides it will deny job restoration, and explain the reasons for this decision;

3. Offer the employee a reasonable opportunity to return to work from FMLA leave after giving this notice; and

4. Make a final determination as to whether reinstatement will be denied at the end of the leave period if the employee then requests restoration.

In addition to denying reinstatement in certain circumstances to "key" employees, employers are not required to continue FMLA benefits or reinstate employees who would have been laid off or otherwise had their employment terminated had they continued to work during the FMLA leave.

Loss of Right to Reinstatement

Employees who give unequivocal notice that they do not intend to return to work lose their entitlement to FMLA leave. Employees who are unable to return to work and have exhausted their 12 weeks of FMLA leave in the designated "12 month period" no longer have FMLA leave protection or job restoration.

Under certain circumstances, employers who advise employees experiencing a serious health condition that they will require a medical certificate of fitness for duty to return to work may deny reinstatement to an employee who fails to provide the certification, or may delay reinstatement until the certification is submitted.

Violations

It is unlawful for any employer to interfere with, restrain, or deny the exercise of any right provided by the FMLA. It is also unlawful for an employer to discharge or discriminate against any individual for opposing any practice, or because of involvement in any proceeding, related to the FMLA.

The Wage and Hour Division investigates complaints. If violations cannot be satisfactorily resolved, the U.S. Department of Labor may bring action in court to compel compliance. Individuals may also bring a private civil action against an employer for violations.

Employers who violate the Act, including its provisions against retaliating against those who take advantage of its protections, may be required to pay backpay, damages, attorneys' and expert witnesses' fees—and importantly, for the cost of up to 12 weeks of caring for a child, spouse or parent.

State Laws

Just over half the states have also enacted their own leave laws. Most of these laws are nearly identical to the federal provisions. State laws which grant rights that are greater than the FMLA supersede the statute. Thus, the reader is advised to check the law of his or her own jurisdiction.

Employers may also provide family and medical leave that is more generous than the FMLA leave requirements. The FMLA does not modify or affect any Federal or State law which prohibits discrimination.

The text of the Family Medical Leave Act is set forth in the Appendix.

CHAPTER 11:
EMPLOYMENT TERMINATION

In General

Being unemployed is a frightening prospect for many Americans. It is common to open the newspaper and discover major companies engaged in massive lay-offs of thousands of workers. The long-held concept of "job security" is rare. Unless there is an employment agreement for a certain term, an employer can usually discharge or lay off any of its employees, with or without cause, and with or without notice.

For example, an employer can fire an employee for cause—e.g., absenteeism or incompetence—or for reasons unrelated to the employee, such as corporate downsizing, plant closings, etc.

Legal Restrictions

Although an employer basically has the right to hire and fire employees at will, the law does provide some restrictions. As set forth in this almanac, an employer cannot discriminate in making any adverse employment decision, e.g. on the basis of age, race, gender, religion, national origin, or disability. Neither can an employer violate any applicable federal or state laws.

If an employee is discharged or laid off, he or she should examine the circumstances to see whether there was some hidden discriminatory motive for the adverse action. For example, if the employee's pension was close to vesting when he or she was fired, this may signal an age discrimination claim under the ADEA. If a disproportionate number of minority employees were laid off, there may exist a Title VII discrimination claim.

Severance Pay

In order to avoid a lawsuit, many employers will negotiate certain benefits, e.g. severance pay, in return for an employee's waiving their right to sue. Employers are generally not required by law to give severance pay unless a promise to do so was made, e.g. in writing, such as a contract or employment manual; or implied, for example when the employer has a long history of giving severance pay to departing employees.

Health Benefits

Pursuant to the Consolidated Omnibus Budget Reconciliation Act of 1986 (COBRA), employers with 20 or more employees must offer the option of continuation of insurance coverage by the company's group health insurance plan, at the workers' own expense, for a certain amount of time following termination. This continuation of coverage must also include family coverage.

Unemployment Benefits

In order to avoid a financial catastrophe, a discharged or laid off employee should immediately apply for unemployment benefits to offset some of the lost income. There is usually a lag time of several weeks or more before the first check is received. Savings can quickly dissipate under such circumstances.

Benefits under state unemployment insurance programs are generally paid for approximately 26 weeks in most states. The income amount is calculated as a percentage of the employee's former wages.

CHAPTER 12:
EMPLOYEE PENSION AND RETIREMENT BENEFITS

Employee Pension Plans

In General

An employee pension plan is a program established and maintained by an employer primarily to provide systematically for the payment of benefits to an employee, or the employee's beneficiaries, over a period of years after the employee's retirement. The amount of the retirement benefits paid by the pension plan is based on such factors as the number of years employed, and wages.

Eligibility

If an employer offers a pension plan, there are certain criteria the employee must generally meet in order to receive retirement benefits, such as length of employment, and age at retirement. Employees should familiarize themselves with all aspects of the employer's pension plan so that they can best plan for retirement. Unlike Social Security retirement benefits, pension benefits are often taxable income to recipients.

Vesting

Some pension plans are *vested* plans. This means that plan participants are guaranteed payment, even if they choose to leave their employment. If pension rights are fully vested, the employee is usually entitled to receive their full pension, based on their length of service, when leaving his or her place of employment.

If the pension plan is *partially vested*, the employee is entitled to receive partial pension benefits upon leaving his or her employment before retirement age. If the pension plan is *not vested*, however, the employee will not receive anything upon leaving, except repayment of the employee's own contributions to the plan, if any were made.

The Employee Retirement Income Security Act of 1974

In 1974, Congress enacted the *Employee Retirement Income Security Act of 1974 (ERISA)*. ERISA was enacted to protect the interests of employees in connection with their pension plans and other work-related benefits.

The statute is complex, but employees should be aware of its basic provisions.

Under ERISA, those who are responsible for operating a retirement plan, known as plan administrators, are obligated to provide employees with important facts about the employer's pension plan, in writing and free of charge. ERISA also requires employers to provide vesting rights within certain specified time limits, although an employer can grant vesting rights earlier.

Under ERISA, employers are given three alternatives to comply with the vesting requirement:

1. Ten Year Vesting - Full vesting is achieved after ten years of credited service. This means that your pension will be fully vested after you have worked for your employer for ten years.

2. Graded vesting - This provides for vesting of 25% of benefits after five years of credited service, vesting of an additional 5% per year of benefits after another five years of service, and vesting of an additional 10% for each year thereafter. This means that your plan is 50% vested after ten years of employment, and your plan will be fully vested after fifteen years of employment.

3. Rule 45 Vesting - Vesting according to Rule 45 means that 50% vesting must be given when the total of an employee's age and length of employment equals 45, as long as the length of service is at least five years. In addition, vesting rights increase 10% each year after the 50% level is reached until full vesting is attained. In any event, under Rule 45 vesting, employees must be given their 50% vesting rights after ten years of employment regardless of their age.

Personal Retirement Plans

In General

If one's employer does not provide a pension plan, it would be prudent for the employee to set up his or her own personal retirement account. There are two main types of personal retirement accounts available.

Employees who have no pension plan through their employer may set up what is known as an *Individual Retirement Account (IRA)*. Persons who are self-employed may invest in *Keogh* plans.

IRA and Keogh plans are similar in many ways. They are both retirement plans which the individual funds from their own savings. Both plans afford the investor a tax deferral as an incentive to save money for their retirement. This tax deferral allows the investor to build up savings more quickly.

Any withdrawal from the account will be taxed, but interest earned on the principal is not taxed until retirement. It is worth noting, however, that withdrawals from these accounts will likely only take place after retirement, at which time the investor will probably be in a lower tax bracket.

Another advantage of investing money in an IRA or Keogh plan is that, upon death, the funds in the plan are not subject to probate and go directly to the beneficiary named on the account when it was opened. However, the amount of funds in the plan will be included in the decedent's taxable estate.

Individual Retirement Accounts

The IRA plan has a monetary contribution cap of $2,000 dollars per year provided the investor has earned income of $2,000 or more. If earnings are less than $2,000, the investor can contribute up to the amount earned. There are exceptions to the annual limit under certain situations, e.g. if the investor is married and his or her spouse does not have any earnings.

One additional situation in which contributions to an IRA may be made is where you change jobs before you are ready to retire, and receive a lump sum payment from your former employer's pension plan. In such a case, you may deposit that lump sum into your IRA account regardless of the amount.

Keogh Plans

The Keogh plan, also known as the *H.R. 10* plan, was enacted into law in 1962. The Keogh plan was designed for the self-employed person, and is a retirement vehicle often used by professionals, such as attorneys and physicians, as well as small business organizations.

Unlike the IRA, the Keogh plan allows investors to annually contribute up to $30,000 or 25% of their earned income, whichever is less. There is also a special kind of Keogh plan, called a *defined benefit plan*, to which an investor may make higher annual contributions.

Fees and Penalties

It is important when shopping around for a retirement account to inquire about any applicable fees and commissions. Penalties will be assessed if the investor attempts to withdraw money from the retirement plan before reaching the age of 59-1/2, unless the investor suffers a total disability. However, withdrawals must begin by age 70-1/2 to avoid additional penalties. Of course, any amount withdrawn must be added to one's taxable income for that year. Upon the investor's death, the decedent's heirs can withdraw money from the account without penalty.

Social Security Retirement Income

Social Security is a national program administered by the Social Security Administration, whereby employees and self-employed persons pay contributions, known as social security taxes, into the program during their working years. The amount of these taxes, which is determined by Congress, is a percentage of the employee's gross salary, up to a designated limit. This tax deduction is often designated as "FICA" on the employee's payroll stub. The employer is also required to pay social security taxes based on the employee's gross salary.

Although Social Security is most often thought of as a retirement program, many persons are eligible to receive Social Security benefits before retirement age. When a person's earnings stop or are reduced because he or she retires, dies, or becomes disabled, monthly cash benefits are paid to replace part of the earnings the person or his or her dependent family has lost. Although a person may thus be eligible for Social Security benefits at any age, the majority of Social Security recipients—approximately 60%—receive Social Security retirement benefits due to retirement.

Some senior citizens continue to work full-time beyond full retirement age, and do not sign up for Social Security. Delaying retirement can increase one's Social Security benefit by increasing their average earnings and will earn the employee a special credit from the Social Security program. This credit takes the form of a designated percentage added to the recipient's Social Security benefit depending on his or her date of birth. If an employee continues to work after retirement age while also receiving Social Security, in contrast, the amount of Social Security benefits received may be reduced or eliminated depending on the amount of earnings.

APPENDIX 1:
THE AMERICANS WITH DISABILITIES ACT OF 1990

SECTION 1. SHORT TITLE; TABLE OF CONTENTS

(a) Short Title. This Act may be cited as the Americans with Disabilities Act of 1990.

(b) Table of Contents. (omitted)

SECTION 2. FINDINGS AND PURPOSES

(a) Findings. The Congress finds that

(1) some 43,000,000 Americans have one or more physical or mental disabilities, and this number is increasing as the population as a whole is growing older;

(2) historically, society has tended to isolate and segregate individuals with disabilities, and, despite some improvements, such forms of discrimination against individuals with disabilities continue to be a serious and pervasive social problem;

(3) discrimination against individuals with disabilities persists in such critical areas as employment, housing, public accommodations, education, transportation, communication, recreation, institutionalization, health services, voting, and access to public services;

(4) unlike individuals who have experienced discrimination on the basis of race, color, sex, national origin, religion, or age, individuals who have experienced discrimination on the basis of disability have often had no legal recourse to redress such discrimination;

(5) individuals with disabilities continually encounter various forms of discrimination, including outright intentional exclusion, the discriminatory effects of architectural, transportation, and communication barriers, overprotective rules and policies, failure to make modifications to existing facilities and practices, exclusionary qualification standards and criteria, segregation, and relegation to lesser services, programs, activities, benefits, jobs, or other opportunities;

(6) census data, national polls, and other studies have documented that people with disabilities, as a group, occupy an inferior status in our society, and are severely disadvantaged socially, vocationally, economically, and educationally;

(7) individuals with disabilities are a discrete and insular minority who have been faced with restrictions and limitations, subjected to a history of purposeful unequal treatment, and relegated to a position of political powerlessness in our society, based on characteristics that are beyond the control of such individuals and resulting from stereotypic assumptions not truly indicative of the individual ability of such individuals to participate in, and contribute to, society;

(8) the Nations proper goals regarding individuals with disabilities are to assure equality of opportunity, full participation, independent living, and economic self-sufficiency for such individuals; and

(9) the continuing existence of unfair and unnecessary discrimination and prejudice denies people with disabilities the opportunity to compete on an equal basis and to pursue those opportunities for which our free society is justifiably famous, and costs the United States billions of dollars in unnecessary expenses resulting from dependency and nonproductivity.

(b) Purpose. It is the purpose of this Act

(1) to provide a clear and comprehensive national mandate for the elimination of discrimination against individuals with disabilities;

(2) to provide clear, strong, consistent, enforceable standards addressing discrimination against individuals with disabilities;

(3) to ensure that the Federal Government plays a central role in enforcing the standards established in this Act on behalf of individuals with disabilities; and

(4) to invoke the sweep of congressional authority, including the power to enforce the fourteenth amendment and to regulate commerce, in order to address the major areas of discrimination faced day-to-day by people with disabilities.

TITLE I: EMPLOYMENT

SECTION 101. DEFINITIONS

As used in this title:

(1) Commission. The term Commission means the Equal Employment Opportunity Commission established by section 705 of the Civil Rights Act of 1964 (42 U.S.C. 2000e- 4).

(2) Covered entity. The term covered entity means an employer, employment agency, labor organization, or joint labor-management committee.

(3) Direct threat. The term direct threat means a significant risk to the health or safety of others that cannot be eliminated by reasonable accommodation.

(4) Employee. The term employee means an individual employed by an employer. With respect to employment in a foreign country, such term includes an individual who is a citizen of the United States.

(5) Employer.

(A) In general. The term employer means a person engaged in an industry affecting commerce who has 15 or more employees for each working day in each of 20 or more calendar weeks in the current or preceding calendar year, and any agent of such person, except that, for two years following the effective date of this title, an employer means a person engaged in an industry affecting commerce who has 25 or more employees for each working day in each of 20 or more calendar weeks in the current or preceding year, and any agent of such person.

(B) Exceptions. The term employer does not include

(i) the United States, a corporation wholly owned by the government of the United States, or an Indian tribe; or

(ii) a bona fide private membership club (other than a labor organization) that is exempt from taxation under section 501(c) of the Internal Revenue Code of 1986.

(6) Illegal use of drugs.

(A) In general. The term illegal use of drugs means the use of drugs, the possession or distribution of which is unlawful under the Controlled Substances Act (21 U.S.C. 812). Such term does not include the use of a drug taken under supervision by a licensed health care professional, or other uses authorized by the Controlled Substances Act or other provisions of Federal law.

(B) Drugs. The term drug means a controlled substance, as defined in schedules I through V of section 202 of the Controlled Substances Act.

(7) Person, etc. The terms person , labor organization , employment agency, commerce, and industry affecting commerce, shall have the

same meaning given such terms in section 701 of the Civil Rights Act of 1964 (42 U.S.C. 2000e).

(8) Qualified individual with a disability. The term qualified individual with a disability means an individual with a disability who, with or without reasonable accommodation, can perform the essential functions of the employment position that such individual holds or desires. For the purposes of this title, consideration shall be given to the employers judgment as to what functions of a job are essential, and if an employer has prepared a written description before advertising or interviewing applicants for the job, this description shall be considered evidence of the essential functions of the job.

(9) Reasonable accommodation. The term reasonable accommodation may include

(A) making existing facilities used by employees readily accessible to and usable by individuals with disabilities; and

(B) job restructuring, part-time or modified work schedules, reassignment to a vacant position, acquisition or modification of equipment or devices, appropriate adjustment or modifications of examinations, training materials or policies, the provision of qualified readers or interpreters, and other similar accommodations for individuals with disabilities.

(10) Undue hardship.

(A) In general. The term undue hardship means an action requiring significant difficulty or expense, when considered in light of the factors set forth in subparagraph (B).

(B) Factors to be considered. In determining whether an accommodation would impose an undue hardship on a covered entity, factors to be considered include

(i) the nature and cost of the accommodation needed under this Act;

(ii) the overall financial resources of the facility or facilities involved in the provision of the reasonable accommodation; the number of persons employed at such facility; the effect on expenses and resources, or the impact otherwise of such accommodation upon the operation of the facility;

(iii) the overall financial resources of the covered entity; the overall size of the business of a covered entity with respect to the number of its employees; the number, type, and location of its facilities; and

(iv) the type of operation or operations of the covered entity, including the composition, structure, and functions of the workforce of such entity; the geographic separateness, administrative, or fiscal relationship of the facility or facilities in question to the covered entity.

SECTION 102. DISCRIMINATION

(a) General Rule. No covered entity shall discriminate against a qualified individual with a disability because of the disability of such individual in regard to job application procedures, the hiring, advancement, or discharge of employees, employee compensation, job training, and other terms, conditions, and privileges of employment.

(b) Construction. As used in subsection (a), the term discriminate includes

(1) limiting, segregating, or classifying a job applicant or employee in a way that adversely affects the opportunities or status of such applicant or employee because of the disability of such applicant or employee;

(2) participating in a contractual or other arrangement or relationship that has the effect of subjecting a covered entity's qualified applicant or employee with a disability to the discrimination prohibited by this title (such relationship includes a relationship with an employment or referral agency, labor union, an organization providing fringe benefits to an employee of the covered entity, or an organization providing training and apprenticeship programs);

(3) utilizing standards, criteria, or methods of administration

(A) that have the effect of discrimination on the basis of disability; or

(B) that perpetuate the discrimination of others who are subject to common administrative control;

(4) excluding or otherwise denying equal jobs or benefits to a qualified individual because of the known disability of an individual with whom the qualified individual is known to have a relationship or association;

(5) (A) not making reasonable accommodations to the known physical or mental limitations of an otherwise qualified individual with a disability who is an applicant or employee, unless such covered entity can

demonstrate that the accommodation would impose an undue hardship on the operation of the business of such covered entity; or

(B) denying employment opportunities to a job applicant or employee who is an otherwise qualified individual with a disability, if such denial is based on the need of such covered entity to make reasonable accommodation to the physical or mental impairments of the employee or applicant;

(6) using qualification standards, employment tests or other selection criteria that screen out or tend to screen out an individual with a disability or a class of individuals with disabilities unless the standard, test or other selection criteria, as used by the covered entity, is shown to be job-related for the position in question and is consistent with business necessity; and

(7) failing to select and administer tests concerning employment in the most effective manner to ensure that, when such test is administered to a job applicant or employee who has a disability that impairs sensory, manual, or speaking skills, such test results accurately reflect the skills, aptitude, or whatever other factor of such applicant or employee that such test purports to measure, rather than reflecting the impaired sensory, manual, or speaking skills of such employee or applicant (except where such skills are the factors that the test purports to measure).

(c) Covered Entities in Foreign Countries.

(1) In general. It shall not be unlawful under this section for a covered entity to take any action that constitutes discrimination under this section with respect to an employee in a workplace in a foreign country if compliance with this section would cause such covered entity to violate the law of the foreign country in which such workplace is located.

(2) Control of Corporation.

(A) Presumption. If an employer controls a corporation whose place of incorporation is a foreign country, any practice that constitutes discrimination under this section and is engaged in by such corporation shall be presumed to be engaged in by such employer.

(B) Exception. This section shall not apply with respect to the foreign operations of an employer that is a foreign person not controlled by an American employer.

(C) Determination. For purposes of this paragraph, the determination of whether an employer controls a corporation shall be based on -

(i) the interrelation of operations;

(ii) the common management;

(iii) the centralized control of labor relations; and

(iv) the common ownership or financial control of the employer and the corporation.

(d) Medical Examinations and Inquiries.

(1) In general. The prohibition against discrimination as referred to in subsection (a) shall include medical examinations and inquiries.

(2) Preemployment.

(A) Prohibited examination or inquiry. Except as provided in paragraph (3), a covered entity shall not conduct a medical examination or make inquiries of a job applicant as to whether such applicant is an individual with a disability or as to the nature or severity of such disability.

(B) Acceptable inquiry. A covered entity may make preemployment inquiries into the ability of an applicant to perform job-related functions.

(3) Employment entrance examination. A covered entity may require a medical examination after an offer of employment has been made to a job applicant and prior to the commencement of the employment duties of such applicant, and may condition an offer of employment on the results of such examination, if

(A) all entering employees are subjected to such an examination regardless of disability;

(B) information obtained regarding the medical condition or history of the applicant is collected and maintained on separate forms and in separate medical files and is treated as a confidential medical record, except that

(i) supervisors and managers may be informed regarding necessary restrictions on the work or duties of the employee and necessary accommodations;

(ii) first aid and safety personnel may be informed, when appropriate, if the disability might require emergency treatment; and

(iii) government officials investigating compliance with this Act shall be provided relevant information on request; and

(C) the results of such examination are used only in accordance with this title.

(4) Examination and inquiry.

(A) Prohibited examinations and inquiries. A covered entity shall not require a medical examination and shall not make inquiries of an employee as to whether such employee is an individual with a disability or as to the nature or severity of the disability, unless such examination or inquiry is shown to be job-related and consistent with business necessity.

(B) Acceptable examinations and inquiries. A covered entity may conduct voluntary medical examinations, including voluntary medical histories, which are part of an employee health program available to employees at that work site. A covered entity may make inquiries into the ability of an employee to perform job-related functions.

(C) Requirement. Information obtained under subparagraph (B) regarding the medical condition or history of any employee are subject to the requirements of subparagraphs (B) and (C) of paragraph (3).

SECTION 103. DEFENSES

(a) In General. It may be a defense to a charge of discrimination under this Act that an alleged application of qualification standards, tests, or selection criteria that screen out or tend to screen out or otherwise deny a job or benefit to an individual with a disability has been shown to be job-related and consistent with business necessity, and such performance cannot be accomplished by reasonable accommodation, as required under this title.

(b) Qualification Standards. The term qualification standards may include a requirement that an individual shall not pose a direct threat to the health or safety of other individuals in the workplace.

(c) Religious Entities.

(1) In general. This title shall not prohibit a religious corporation, association, educational institution, or society from giving preference in

employment to individuals of a particular religion to perform work connected with the carrying on by such corporation, association, educational institution, or society of its activities.

(2) Religious tenets requirement. Under this title, a religious organization may require that all applicants and employees conform to the religious tenets of such organization.

(d) List of Infectious and Communicable Diseases.

(1) In general. The Secretary of Health and Human Services, not later than 6 months after the date of enactment of this Act, shall

(A) review all infectious and communicable diseases which may be transmitted through handling the food supply;

(B) publish a list of infectious and communicable diseases which are transmitted through handling the food supply;

(C) publish the methods by which such diseases are transmitted; and

(D) widely disseminate such information regarding the list of diseases and their modes of transmissibility to the general public. Such list shall be updated annually.

(2) Applications. In any case in which an individual has an infectious or communicable disease that is transmitted to others through the handling of food, that is included on the list developed by the Secretary of Health and Human Services under paragraph (1), and which cannot be eliminated by reasonable accommodation, a covered entity may refuse to assign or continue to assign such individual to a job involving food handling.

(3) Construction. Nothing in this Act shall be construed to preempt, modify, or amend any State, county, or local law, ordinance, or regulation applicable to food handling which is designed to protect the public health from individuals who pose a significant risk to the health or safety of others, which cannot be eliminated by reasonable accommodation, pursuant to the list of infectious or communicable diseases and the modes of transmissibility published by the Secretary of Health and Human Services.

SECTION 104. ILLEGAL USE OF DRUGS AND ALCOHOL

(a) Qualified Individual With a Disability. For purposes of this title, the term qualified individual with a disability shall not include any employee or applicant who is currently engaging in the illegal use of drugs, when the covered entity acts on the basis of such use.

(b) Rules of Construction. Nothing in subsection (a) shall be construed to exclude as a qualified individual with a disability an individual who

(1) has successfully completed a supervised drug rehabilitation program and is no longer engaging in the illegal use of drugs, or has otherwise been rehabilitated successfully and is no longer engaging in such use;

(2) is participating in a supervised rehabilitation program and is no longer engaging in such use; or

(3) is erroneously regarded as engaging in such use, but is not engaging in such use; except that it shall not be a violation of this Act for a covered entity to adopt or administer reasonable policies or procedures, including but not limited to drug testing, designed to ensure that an individual described in paragraph (1) or (2) is no longer engaging in the illegal use of drugs.

(c) Authority of Covered Entity. A covered entity

(1) may prohibit the illegal use of drugs and the use of alcohol at the workplace by all employees;

(2) may require that employees shall not be under the influence of alcohol or be engaging in the illegal use of drugs at the workplace;

(3) may require that employees behave in conformance with the requirements established under the Drug-Free Workplace Act of 1988 (41 U.S.C. 701 et seq.);

(4) may hold an employee who engages in the illegal use of drugs or who is an alcoholic to the same qualification standards for employment or job performance and behavior that such entity holds other employees, even if any unsatisfactory performance or behavior is related to the drug use or alcoholism of such employee; and

(5) may, with respect to Federal regulations regarding alcohol and the illegal use of drugs, require that

(A) employees comply with the standards established in such regulations of the Department of Defense, if the employees of the covered entity are employed in an industry subject to such regulations, including complying with regulations (if any) that apply to employment in sensitive positions in such an industry, in the case of employees of the covered entity who are employed in such positions (as defined in the regulations of the Department of Defense);

(B) employees comply with the standards established in such regulations of the Nuclear Regulatory Commission, if the employees of the covered entity are employed in an industry subject to such regulations, including complying with regulations (if any) that apply to employment in sensitive positions in such an industry, in the case of employees of the covered entity who are employed in such positions (as defined in the regulations of the Nuclear Regulatory Commission); and

(C) employees comply with the standards established in such regulations of the Department of Transportation, if the employees of the covered entity are employed in a transportation industry subject to such regulations, including complying with such regulations (if any) that apply to employment in sensitive positions in such an industry, in the case of employees of the covered entity who are employed in such positions (as defined in the regulations of the Department of Transportation).

(d) Drug Testing.

(1) In general. For purposes of this title, a test to determine the illegal use of drugs shall not be considered a medical examination.

(2) Construction. Nothing in this title shall be construed to encourage, prohibit, or authorize the conducting of drug testing for the illegal use of drugs by job applicants or employees or making employment decisions based on such test results.

(e) Transportation Employees. Nothing in this title shall be construed to encourage, prohibit, restrict, or authorize the otherwise lawful exercise by entities subject to the jurisdiction of the Department of Transportation of authority to

(1) test employees of such entities in, and applicants for, positions involving safety-sensitive duties for the illegal use of drugs and for on-duty impairment by alcohol; and

(2) remove such persons who test positive for illegal use of drugs and on-duty impairment by alcohol pursuant to paragraph (1) from safety-sensitive duties in implementing subsection (c).

SECTION 105. POSTING NOTICES

Every employer, employment agency, labor organization, or joint labor-management committee covered under this title shall post notices in an accessible format to applicants, employees, and members describing the applicable provisions of this Act, in the manner prescribed by section 711 of the Civil Rights Act of 1964 (42 U.S.C. 2000e- 10).

SECTION 106. REGULATIONS

Not later than 1 year after the date of enactment of this Act, the Commission shall issue regulations in an accessible format to carry out this title in accordance with subchapter II of chapter 5 of title 5, United States Code.

SECTION 107. ENFORCEMENT

(a) Powers, Remedies, and Procedures. The powers, remedies, and procedures set forth in sections 705, 706, 707, 709, and 710 of the Civil Rights Act of 1964 (42 U.S.C. 2000e- 4, 2000e-5, 2000e- 6, 2000e- 8, and 2000e-9) shall be the powers, remedies, and procedures this title provides to the Commission, to the Attorney General, or to any person alleging discrimination on the basis of disability in violation of any provision of this Act, or regulations promulgated under section 106, concerning employment.

(b) Coordination. The agencies with enforcement authority for actions which allege employment discrimination under this title and under the Rehabilitation Act of 1973 shall develop procedures to ensure that administrative complaints filed under this title and under the Rehabilitation Act of 1973 are dealt with in a manner that avoids duplication of effort and prevents imposition of inconsistent or conflicting standards for the same requirements under this title and the Rehabilitation Act of 1973. The Commission, the Attorney General, and the Office of Federal Contract Compliance Programs shall establish such coordinating mechanisms (similar to provisions contained in the joint regulations promulgated by the Commission and the Attorney General at part 42 of title 28 and part 1691 of title 29, Code of Federal Regulations, and the Memorandum of Understanding between the Commission and the Office of Federal Contract Compliance Programs dated January 16, 1981 (46 Fed. Reg. 7435, January 23, 1981)) in regulations implementing this title and Rehabilitation Act of 1973 not later than 18 months after the date of enactment of this Act.

SECTION 108. EFFECTIVE DATE

This title shall become effective 24 months after the date of enactment.

APPENDIX 2:
DIRECTORY OF STATE GOVERNORS' COMMITTEES ON EMPLOYMENT OF THE DISABLED

STATE	DEPARTMENT	ADDRESS	TELEPHONE	FAX
ALABAMA	Governor's Committee on Employment of People with Disabilities, Department of Rehabilitation Service	P.O. Box 11586, 2129 East South Boulevard, Montgomery, AL 36111-0586	(334) 281-8780	(334) 288-1104
ALASKA	Governor's Committee on Employment of People with Disabilities	3301 Eagles Street, Suite 203, Anchorage, AK 99510-7018	(907) 269-4877	(907) 269-4879
ARIZONA	Governor's Committee on Employment of People with Disabilities	1012 E. Willetta, Phoenix, AZ 85006	(602) 239-4762	(602) 239-5256
ARKANSAS	Governor's Commission on People with Disabilities	1616 Brookwood Drive, Little Rock AR 72202	(501) 296-1626	(501) 296-1655
CALIFORNIA	The California Governor's Committee for Employment Disabled Persons	800 Capitol Mall Room 5078 MIC 41, Sacramento, CA 95814	(916) 654-8055	(916) 654-9821
COLORADO	Colorado Governor's Advisory Council for People with Disabilities c/o Aging and Adult Services	110 16th Street Denver, CO 80202	(303) 313-8666	(303) 620-4191

STATE	DEPARTMENT	ADDRESS	TELEPHONE	FAX
CONNECTI-CUT	Governor's Committee on Employment of People with Disabilities, Labor Department	Building, 200 Folly Brook Boulevard, Wethersfield, CT 06109	(203) 566-8061	(203) 566-1519
DELAWARE	Governor's Committee on Employment of People with Disabilities	4425 North Market Street, Wilmington, DE 19809-0969	(302) 761-8275	(302) 761-6611
DISTRICT OF COLUMBIA	Mayor's Committee on Persons with Disabilities	800 Ninth Street S.W., 4th Floor, Washington, D.C. 20024	(202) 645-5729	(202) 645-0840
FLORIDA	Florida Governor's Alliance for the Employment of Disabled Citizens, Inc.	346 Office Plaza Drive, Tallahassee, FL 32301-2808	(904) 942-7266	(904) 942-1728
GEORGIA	Georgia Committee on Employment of Persons with Disabilities Division of Rehabilitation Service, Director's Office	2 Peachtree Street N.W., 23rd Floor, Atlanta, GA 30303	(404) 657-3005	(404) 657-3079
HAWAII	Commission on Persons with Disabilities	919 Ala Moana Blvd., Suite 101, Honolulu HI 96814	(808) 586-8121	(808) 586-8129
IDAHO	Governor's Committee on Employment of People with Disabilities Department of Employment	317 Main Street, Boise, ID 83735	(208) 334-6469	(208) 334-6300
ILLINOIS	Department of Rehabilitative Services	100 West Randolph St., Suite 8-100, Chicago, IL 60601	(312) 814-5081	(312) 814-4430

STATE	DEPARTMENT	ADDRESS	TELEPHONE	FAX
INDIANA	Governor's Commission on Planning for People with Disabilities	143 West Market Street, Indianapolis IN 46204	(317) 232-7773	(317) 233-3712
IOWA	Iowa Commission of Persons with Disabilities Department of Human Rights	Lucas State Office Building, 321 East 12th Street, Des Moines IA 50319	(515) 281-5969	(515) 242-6119
KANSAS	Kansas Commission on Disability Concerns	1430 S.W. Topeka Avenue, Topeka, KS 66612-1877	(913) 296-1722	(913) 296-0466
KENTUCKY	Kentucky Committee on Employment of People with Disabilities	275 E. Main Street, Frankfort, KY 40621	(502) 564-2918	(502) 564-7452
LOUISIANA	Governor's Office of Disability Affairs Office of the Governor	P.O. Box 94004, Baton Rouge, LA 70806-9004	(504) 342-7015	(504) 342-7099
MAINE	Governor's Committee on Employment of People with Disabilities	35 Anthony Avenue, Augusta, ME 04330	(207) 624-5307	(207) 624-5302
MARYLAND	Governor's Committee on Employment of People with Disabilities	300 West Lexington Street, Baltimore, MD 21201	(410) 333-2263	(410) 333-6674
MASSACHU-SETTS	Governor's Commission on Employment of People with Disabilities	Department of Employment and Training Policy Office 19 Stanford Street, 4th Floor, Boston, MA 02114	(617) 626-5180	(617) 727-8014
MICHIGAN	Michigan Commission on Disability Concerns	320 No. Washington Square, Suite 250, Lansing, MI 48909	(517) 334-8000	(517) 334-6637

STATE	DEPARTMENT	ADDRESS	TELEPHONE	FAX
MINNESOTA	Minnesota State Council on Disability	121 E. 7th Place, Suite 107, St. Paul, MN 55101	(612) 296-1743	(612) 296-5935
MISSISSIPPI	Mississippi Department of Rehabilitation Services	P.O. Box 1698, Jackson, MS 39215-1698	(601) 853-5100	(601) 853-5325
MISSOURI	Missouri Governor's Council on Disability	3315 West Truman Boulevard, Jefferson City MO 65102	(573) 751-2600	(573) 751-2600
MONTANA	Governor's Advisory Council on Disability	State Personnel Division, Dept. of Administration P.O. Box 200127, Helena, MT 59620-0127	(406) 444-3794	(406) 444-0544
NEBRASKA	Governor's Committee on Employment of People with Disabilities	Nebraska Job Service, Dept. of Labor 550 South 16th Street, Box 94600, Lincoln, NE 68509	(402) 471-2776	(402) 471-2318
NEVADA	Governor's Committee on Employment of People with Disabilities	4001 S. Virginia Street Reno, NV 89502	(702) 688-1111	(702) 688-1113
NEW HAMPSHIRE	Governor's Commission on Disability	57 Regional Drive, Concord, NH 03301-8518	(603) 271-2773	(603) 271-2837
NEW JERSEY	New Jersey Division of Vocational Rehabilitation Services	CN 398 Trenton, NJ 08625	(609) 292-7959	(609) 292-8347
NEW MEXICO	Governor's Committee on Concerns of the Handicapped	491 Old Santa Fe Trail, Santa Fe, NM 87501	(505) 827-6465	(505) 827-6328
NEW YORK	New York State Office of Advocate for Persons with Disabilities	One Empire State Plaza, Suite 1001, Albany, NY 12223-1150	(518) 473-4129	(518) 473-6005

STATE	DEPARTMENT	ADDRESS	TELEPHONE	FAX
NORTH CAROLINA	Governor's Advocacy Council for Persons with Disabilities Office of the ADA	2113 Cameron Street, Suite 218, Raleigh, NC 27605-1344	(919) 733-9250	(919) 733-9173
NORTH DAKOTA	Governor's Committee on Employment of People with Disabilities	600 South 2nd Street, Bismarck, ND 58504	(701) 328-8952	(701) 328-8989
OHIO	Ohio Governor's Council on People with Disabilities	400 East Campus View Boulevard, Columbus, OH 43235-4604	(614) 438-1393	(614) 438-1274
OKLAHOMA	Governor's Committee on Employment of the Handicapped Office of Handicapped Concerns	2712 Villa Prom Oklahoma City, OK 73107-2423	(405) 521-3756	405) 943-7550
OREGON	Oregon Disabilities Commission	1257 Ferry Street S.E., Salem, OR 97310	(503) 378-3142	(503) 378-3599
PENNSYLVA- NIA	Governor's Committee on Employment of People with Disabilities	Labor and Industry Building, 7th and Forster Streets, Room 1315, Harrisburg, PA 17120	(717) 787-5232	(717) 783-5221
RHODE ISLAND	Governor's Commission on the Handicapped	555 Valley Street, Providence, RI 02908-5686	(401) 277-3731	(401) 277-2833
SOUTH CAROLINA	Governor's Committee on Employment of the Handicapped Vocational Rehabilitation Department	1410 Boston Avenue, West Columbia, SC 29171-0015	(803) 896-6581	(803) 896-6510
SOUTH DAKOTA	Governor's Advisory Committee on Employment of People with Disabilities	Department of Human Services 221 South Central, Suite 34 A, Pierre, SD 57501	(605) 945-2207	(605) 945-2422

STATE	DEPARTMENT	ADDRESS	TELEPHONE	FAX
TENNESSEE	Tennessee Committee for Employment of People with Disabilities	Division of Rehabilitation Services 400 Deaderick Street, Nashville, TN 37219	(615) 313-4891	(615) 741-6508
TEXAS	Governor's Committee on People with Disabilities	1100 San Jacinto, Room 300, Austin, TX 78701	(512) 463-5739	(512) 463-5745
UTAH	Utah Governor's Committee on Employment of People with Disabilities	4490 South 2700 East, Salt Lake City, UT 84124	(801) 278-8733	(801) 532-2434
VERMONT	Governor's Committee on Employment of People with Disabilities	103 South Main Street, Waterbury, VT 05671-0206	(802) 241-2612	(802) 241-2979
VIRGINIA	The Virginia Board for People with Disabilities,	P.O. Box 613, Richmond, VA 23205-0613	(804) 786-0016	(804) 786-1118
WASHING-TON	Governor's Committee on Disability Issues and Employment	605 Woodland Square Loop SE, 3rd Floor, Olympia, WA 98507-9046	(360) 438-3168	(360) 438-3208
WEST VIRGINIA	Division of Rehabilitation Services	State Capitol Building, P.O. Box 50890, Charleston, WV 25305	(304) 766-2680	(304) 766-2690
WISCONSIN	Governor's Committee for People with Disabilities Client Assistance Program	P.O. Box 7850, Madison, WI 53707-7850	(608) 266-5378	(608) 267-0949
WYOMING	Governor's Committee on Employment of People with Disabilities	1st Floor - East Wing, Herschler Building, Room 1126, Cheyenne, WY 82002	(307) 777-7191	(307) 777-5939

APPENDIX 3:
TABLE OF STATE MINIMUM WAGE LAWS

STATE	MINIMUM WAGE LAW	BASIC MINIMUM HOURLY RATE	PREMIUM PAY AFTER REGULAR HOURS
ALABAMA	No	N/A	N/A
ALASKA	Yes	$5.65[1]	8 hours per day/40 hours per week[2]
ARIZONA	No	N/A/	N/A
ARKANSAS	Yes[3]	$5.15	40 hours per week.
CALIFORNIA	Yes	$5.15, $5.75 eff. 3/1/98	8 hours per day and double time for over 12 hours per day/40 hours per week, after 7th day, the first 8 hours is at time and one-half, and over 8 hours is at double time rate.[4]
COLORADO	Yes	$4.75[5]	12 hours per day/40 hours per week
CONNECTICUT	Yes	$5.18[6]	40 hours per week.[7]
DELAWARE	Yes	$5.15[8]	
DISTRICT OF COLUMBIA	Yes	$6.15[9]	40 hours per week.
FLORIDA	No	N/A	N/A
GEORGIA	Yes[10]	$3.25	
HAWAII	Yes[11]	$5.25	40 hours per week.
IDAHO	Yes	$5.15	40 hours per week.
ILLINOIS	Yes[12]	$5.15[13]	40 hours per week.
INDIANA	Yes[14]	$3.35	
IOWA	Yes	$5.15[15]	
KANSAS	Yes[16]	$2.65	40 hours per week.

STATE	MINIMUM WAGE LAW	BASIC MINIMUM HOURLY RATE	PREMIUM PAY AFTER REGULAR HOURS
KENTUCKY	Yes	$4.25	40 hours per week/7th day[17]
LOUISIANA	No	N/A	N/A
MAINE	Yes	$5.15[18]	40 hours per week.
MARYLAND	Yes[19]	$5.15[20]	40 hours per week.[21]
MASSACHUSETTS	Yes	$5.25	40 hours per week.
MICHIGAN	Yes[22]	$5.25	40 hours per week.
MINNESOTA	Yes	$5.15[23]	48 hours per week.
MISSISSIPPI	No	N/A	N/A
MISSOURI	Yes[24]	$5.15[25]	40 hours per week.
MONTANA	Yes[26]	$5.15[27]	40 hours per week.
NEBRASKA	Yes[28]	$5.15	
NEVADA	Yes	$5.15[29]	8 hours per day/40 hours per week[30]
NEW HAMPSHIRE	Yes	$5.15[31]	40 hours per week.
NEW JERSEY	Yes	$5.05	40 hours per week.
NEW MEXICO	Yes	$4.25	40 hours per week.
NEW YORK	Yes	$4.25	40 hours per week.
NORTH CAROLINA	Yes[32]	$5.15	40 hours per week.[33]
NORTH DAKOTA	Yes	$5.15	40 hours per week.
OHIO	Yes	$4.25[34]	40 hours per week.
OKLAHOMA	Yes[35]	$5.15[36]	
OREGON	Yes	$5.50, $ 6.00 eff. 1/1/98, $6.50 eff. 1/1/99	40 hours per week.[37]
PENNSYLVANIA	Yes	$5.15[38]	40 hours per week.
RHODE ISLAND	Yes	$5.15	40 hours per week.[39]
SOUTH CAROLINA	No	N/A	N/A

STATE	MINIMUM WAGE LAW	BASIC MINIMUM HOURLY RATE	PREMIUM PAY AFTER REGULAR HOURS
SOUTH DAKOTA	Yes	$5.15	
TENNESSEE	No	N/A	N/A
TEXAS	Yes[40]	$3.35,	
UTAH	Yes[41]	$5.15[42]	
VERMONT	Yes[43]	$5.25[44]	40 hours per week[45]
VIRGINIA	Yes[46]	$5.15[47]	
WASHINGTON	Yes	$4.90	40 hours per week.[48]
WEST VIRGINIA	Yes[49]	$4.75, $5.15 eff. 9/1/98	40 hours per week.
WISCONSIN	Yes	$5.15	40 hours per week.
WYOMING	Yes	$1.60	The overtime premium rate is one and one-half times the employee's regular rate unless otherwise specified.[50]

ENDNOTES

1. Alaska's minimum wage rate is automatically set at 50 cents above the rate set in the Fair Labor Standards Act.

2. If there is a signed agreement approved and filed with the Alaska Department of Labor, a 10-hour day, 40-hour workweek may be instituted with premium pay after 10 hours per day instead of 8. The premium overtime pay requirement is not applicable to employers of fewer than 4 employees.

3. Minimum wage rate only applies to employers of 4 or more employees. State law excludes any employment that is subject to the Federal Fair Labor Standards Act.

4. Under specific rules, a 10 or 12-hour day may be instituted without premium pay after 8 hours, but overtime pay at applicable premium rates is required after 40 hours per week and for hours or days in excess of scheduled hours or days. Premium pay is required after 56 hours per week in ski establishments; after 54 hours per week for organized camp counselors and

certain other day-care provider occupations; and after 14 hours per day in the motion picture industry under specified circumstances. Premium pay on 7th day is not required for employees whose total weekly work hours do not exceed 30 and whose total hours in any one work day thereof does not exceed 6.

5. State rate is applicable to businesses not covered by the Federal minimum wage law. Workers under age 20 who are being supported by parents or guardians may be paid $4.25 per hour for the first 90 days of employment.

6. The Connecticut minimum wage rate automatically increases to 1/2 of 1 percent above the rate set in the Fair Labor Standards Act if the Federal minimum wage rate equals or becomes higher than the State minimum.

7. In restaurants and hotel restaurants, for the 7th consecutive day of work, premium pay is required at time and one-half the minimum rate.

8. The Delaware minimum wage is automatically replaced with the Federal minimum wage rate if it is higher than the State minimum.

9. The District of Columbia minimum wage is automatically set at $1.00 above the Federal minimum wage rate.

10. Minimum wage is applicable to employers of 6 or more employees. The State law excludes from coverage any employment that is subject to the Federal Fair Labor Standards Act.

11. An employee earning a guaranteed monthly compensation of $1250 or more is exempt from the State minimum wage law. The State law excludes from coverage any employment that is subject to the Federal Fair Labor Standards Act unless the State wage rate is higher than the Federal.

12. The minimum wage is applicable to employers of 4 or more employees.

13. The Illinois state minimum wage law adopts the Federal minimum wage rate by reference.

14. The minimum wage is applicable to employers of 2 or more employees. The State law excludes from coverage any employment that is subject to the Federal Fair Labor Standards Act.

15. The Iowa minimum wage is automatically replaced with the Federal minimum wage rate if it is higher than the State minimum.

16. The state law excludes from coverage any employment that is subject to the Federal Fair Labor Standards Act.

17. The 7th day overtime law, which is separate from the minimum wage law, differs in coverage from that in the minimum wage law and requires premium pay to those employees who have worked 40 hours in the six previous days.

18. The Maine minimum wage is automatically replaced with the Federal minimum wage rate if it is higher than the State minimum.

19. The Baltimore City Ordinance applies to employers of 2 or more employees.

20. The Maryland state minimum wage adopts the Federal minimum wage rate by reference.

21. Premium pay is required after 48 hours in bowling alleys and for residential employees of institutions, other than hospitals, primarily engaged in the care of the sick, aged, or mentaly ill.

22. The minimum wage rate is applicable to employers of 2 or more employees. The law excludes from coverage any employment that is subject to the Federal Fair Labor Standards Act unless the State wage rate is higher than the Federal.

23. Applies to large employers with annual receipts of $500,000 or more; lesser rate of $4.90 applies to smaller employers.

24. Exemption applies for federally-covered employment and employees of retail or service businesses with gross annual sales or business done of less than $500,000.

25. The state minimum wage law adopts the Federal minimum wage rate by reference.

26. The State law excludes from coverage any employment that is subject to the Federal Fair Labor Standards Act unless the State wage rate is higher than the Federal.

27. The state minimum wage law adopts the Federal minimum wage rate by reference; lesser rate of $4.00 per hour applies to businesses with gross annual sales of $110,000 or less.

28. The minimum wage law is applicable to employers of 4 or more employees.

29. The state minimum wage law adopts the Federal minimum wage rate by reference.

30. By mutual employer/employee agreement, a scheduled 10-hour day for 4 days a week may be worked without premium pay after 8 hours. The premium overtime pay requirement on either a daily or weekly basis is not applicable to employees who are compensated at not less than one and one-half times the minimum rate or to employees or enterprises having a gross annual sales volume of less than $250,000.

31. The New Hampshire minimum wage is automatically replaced with the Federal minimum wage rate if it is higher than the State minimum.

32. The State law excludes from coverage any employment that is subject to the Federal Fair Labor Standards Act unless the State wage rate is higher than the Federal.

33. Premium pay is required after 45 hours a week in seasonal amusements or recreational establishments.

34. Lesser rate of $3.35 applies to employers with gross annual sales from $150,000 to $500,000; and rate of $2.80 applies to employers with gross annual sales under $150,000.

35. The State law excludes from coverage any employment that is subject to the Federal Fair Labor Standards Act.

36. The state minimum wage law adopts the Federal minimum wage rate by reference; applies to employers of 10 or more full-time employees at any one location, and employers with annual gross sales over $100,000 irrespective of number of full-time employees. Lesser rate of $2.00 applies to all other employers.

37. Premium pay required after 10 hours a day in nonfarm canneries, driers, or packing plants and in mills, factories or manufacturing establishments (excluding sawmills, planing mills, shingle mills, and logging camps).

38. The state minimum wage law adopts the Federal minimum wage rate by reference.

39. Time and one-half premium pay for work on Sundays and holidays in retail and certain other businesses is required under two laws that are separate from the minimum wage law. These laws require a license or permit for Sunday/holiday operation that would otherwise be unlawful.

40. The State law excludes from coverage any employment that is subject to the Federal Fair Labor Standards Act.

41. The State law excludes from coverage any employment that is subject to the Federal Fair Labor Standards Act.

42. The state minimum wage law adopts the Federal minimum wage rate by reference.

43. The state minimum wage law applies to employes of 2 or more employees.

44. The Vermont minimum wage is automatically replaced with the Federal minimum wage rate if it is higher than the State minimum.

45. The state overtime pay provision has very limited application because it exempts numerous types of establishments, such as retail and service; seasonal amusement/recreation; hotels, motels, restaurants, and transportation employees to whom the Federal overtime provisions do not apply.

46. The state minimum wage law applies to employers of 4 or more employees and excludes from coverage any employment that is subject to the Federal Fair Labor Standards Act.

47. The state minimum wage law adopts the Federal minimum wage rate by reference.

48. Premium pay not applicable to employees who request compensating time off in lieu of premium pay.

49. State minimum wage law applies to employers of 6 or more employees in one location and excludes from coverage any employment that is subject to the Fedeal Fair Labor Standards Act.

Source: U.S. Department of Labor, Employment Standards Administration.

APPENDIX 4:
DIRECTORY OF DISTRICT OFFICES FOR
THE WAGE AND HOUR DIVISION OF THE EMPLOYMENT
STANDARDS ADMINISTRATION

STATE	DISTRICT	ADDRESS	TELEPHONE	FAX
ALABAMA	Entire State; Nevada -Clark Lincoln & Nye Counties (Las Vegas)	950 North 22nd Street, Suite 656, Birmingham, AL 35203-3711	(205) 731-0666	(205) 731-3482
ALASKA	Entire State	See Seattle, Washington		
ARIZONA	Entire State	3221 North 16th Street, Suite 301, Phoenix, AZ 85016-7103	(602) 640-2990	(602) 640-2979
ARKANSAS	Entire State; Oklahoma	TCBY Building, 425 West Capitol Avenue, Suite 725, Little Rock, AR 72201	(501) 324-5292	(501) 324-5129
CALIFORNIA	Glendale Office	300 South Glendale Avenue, Suite 400, Glendale, CA 91205-1752	(818) 240-5274	(213) 894-6845
CALIFORNIA	Sacramento Office; All of Nevada except Clark, Lincoln & Nye Counties (Las Vegas)	2981 Fulton Avenue, Sacramento, CA 95821	(916) 979-2040	(916) 979-2045
CALIFORNIA	San Diego Office	5675 Ruffin Road, Suite 320, San Diego, CA 92123-1362	(619) 557-5606	(619) 557-6375
CALIFORNIA	San Francisco Office	455 Market Street, Suite 800, San Francisco, CA 94105	(415) 744-5590	(415) 744-5088
COLORADO	Colorado - East of Divide; North Dakota; South Dakota; Wyoming-Albany and Laramie Counties	Federal Office Building, 1961 Stout Street, Room 615, Denver, CO 80294	(303) 844-4405	(303) 844-5532

STATE	DISTRICT	ADDRESS	TELEPHONE	FAX
COLORADO	West of Divide	See Salt Lake City, Utah		
CONNECTI-CUT	Entire State; Rhode Island	135 High Street, Room 310, Hartford, CT 06103	(860) 240-4160	(860) 240-4029
DELAWARE	Entire State	See Baltimore, Maryland		
DISTRICT of COLUMBIA	Entire District	See Baltimore, Maryland		
FLORIDA	Jacksonville Office	3728 Phillips Highway, Suite 219,, Jacksonville, FL 32207	(904) 232-2489	(904) 232-3114
FLORIDA	Miami Office	Sunset Center, 10300 Sunset Drive, Room 255, Miami, FL 33173-3038	(305) 598-6607	(305) 279-8353
FLORIDA	Orlando Office	3444 McCrory Place, Suite 155, Orlando FL 32803-3712	(407) 648-6471	(407) 648-6092
FLORIDA	Tampa Office	Austin Laurel Building, 4905 W. Laurel Avenue, Suite 300, Tampa, FL 33607-3838	(813) 288-1242	(813) 288-1240
GEORGIA	Entire State	Atlanta Federal Center, 61 Forsyth Street S.W., Room 7M10, Atlanta, Ga 30303	(404) 562-2201	(404) 562-2180
HAWAII	Entire State	300 Ala Moana Boulevard, Room 7328,, Honolulu, HI 96850	(808) 541-1361	(808) 541-2956
IDAHO	Northern Panhandle including Coeur d'Alene and Lewiston	See Seattle, Washington Office		
IDAHO	Remainder of State	See Portland, Oregon Office		

STATE	DISTRICT	ADDRESS	TELEPHONE	FAX
ILLINOIS	Chicago Office	230 Dearborn Street, Room 412, Chicago, IL 60604-1595	(312) 353-8145	(312) 353-2327
ILLINOIS	Springfield Office	509 West Capitol Avenue, Suite 205, Springfield, IL 62704-4060	(217) 492-4060	(217) 492-4910
INDIANA	Indianapolis Office	429 N. Pennsylvania Street, Room 403, Indianapolis, IN 46204-1873	(317) 226-6801	(317) 226-5177
INDIANA	South Bend Office	501 E. Monroe, Suite 160, South Bend, IN 46601-1615	(219) 236-8331	(219) 236-8819
IOWA	Entire State	Federal Building, 210 Walnut Street, Room 643, Des Moines, IA 50309	(515) 284-4625	(515) 284-7171
KANSAS	Eastern Third of Kansas; Western Half of Missouri	Gateway Tower II, 400 State Avenue, Suite 706, Kansas City, KS 66101	(913) 551-5721	(913) 551-5730
KANSAS	Remainder of State	See Omaha, Nebraska		
KENTUCKY	Entire State	601 West Broadway, Room 31, Louisville, KY 40202-9570	(502) 582-5226	(502) 582-6890
LOUISIANA	Entire State	701 Loyola Avenue, Room 13028, New Orleans, LA 70113	(504) 589-6171	(504) 589-4751
MAINE	Entire State, See Manchester	New Hampshire		
MARYLAND	Entire State; Delaware; District of Columbia; Northern Virginia; West Virginia - Eastern Panhandle	103 South Gay Street, Room 207, Baltimore, MD 21202-4061	(410) 962-2240	(410) 962-9512

STATE	DISTRICT	ADDRESS	TELEPHONE	FAX
MASSACHU-SETTS	Entire State	JFK Federal Building, Room 525, Boston, MA 02203	(617) 565-2066	
MICHIGAN	Entire State	211 First Street, Detroit, MI 48226-2799	(313) 226-7447	(313) 226-3072
MINNESOTA	Entire State	220 South Second Street, Room 106, Minneapolis, MN 55401	(612) 370-3371	(612) 370-3372
MISSISSIPPI	Entire State	Suite 1020, 188 East Capitol Street, Suite 1020, Jackson, MS 39201-2126	(601) 965-4347	(601) 965-5408
MISSOURI	Eastern Half	1222 Spruce Street, Room 9102B, St. Louis, MO 63101	(314) 539-2706	(314) 539-2723
MISSOURI	Western Half	See Kansas City, Kansas		
MONTANA	Entire State	See Salt Lake City, Utah		
NEBRASKA	Entire State; All of Kansas except Eastern Third	106 South 15th Street, Room 715, Omaha, NE 68102	(402) 221-3719	
NEVADA	Clark, Lincoln & Nye Counties (Las Vegas)	See Phoenix, Arizona		
NEVADA	Remainder of State	See Sacramento, California		
NEW HAMPSHIRE	Entire State; Maine; Vermont	2 Wall Street, 1st Floor, Manchester, NH 03101	(603) 666-7716	(603) 666-7600
NEW JERSEY	Southern New Jersey	3131 Princeton Pike, Building 5 - Room 216, Lawrenceville, NJ 08648	(609) 989-2247	(609) 989-0457

STATE	DISTRICT	ADDRESS	TELEPHONE	FAX
NEW JERSEY	Northern New Jersey	200 Sheffield Street, Suite 102, Mountainside, NJ 07092	(201) 645-2279	(201) 645-2573
NEW MEXICO	Entire State; West Texas -Panhandle including Amarillo, Big Spring, El Paso,, Lubbock, Midland, and Odessa	Western Bank Building, 505 Marquette Avenue N.W., Suite 840, Albuquerque NM 87102- 2160	(505) 248-5115	(505) 248-5119
NEW YORK	Albany Office	Federal Building, Room 822, Albany NY 12207	(518) 431-4278	(518) 431- 4281
NEW YORK	Garden City Office	825 East Gate Boulevard, Room 202, Garden City, NY 11530	(516) 227-3100	(516) 745-0848
NEW YORK	New York City Office	26 Federal Plaza, Room 3838, New York, NY 10278	(212) 264-8185	(212) 264-9548
NORTH CAROLINA	Charlotte Office	800 Briar Creek Road, Suite CC-412, Charlotte, NC 28205-6903	(704) 344-6302	(704) 344-6307
NORTH CAROLINA	Raleigh Office	Somerset Park Building, 4407 Bland Road, Suite 260, Raleigh, NC 27609-6296	(919) 790-2741	(919) 790-2843
NORTH DAKOTA	Entire State	See Denver, Colorado		
OHIO	Cincinnati Office	525 Vine Street, Suite 880, Cincinnati, OH 45202-3268	(513) 684-2908	(513) 684-2906
OHIO	Cleveland Office	Federal Office Building, 1240 East Ninth Street, Room 817, Cleveland, OH 44199-2054	(216) 522-3892	(216) 522-4235

STATE	DISTRICT	ADDRESS	TELEPHONE	FAX
OHIO	Columbus Office	200 North High Street, Room 646, Columbus, OH 43215-2475	(614) 469-5677	(614) 469-5428
OKLAHOMA	Entire State	See Little Rock, Arkansas		
OREGON	Entire State; Southwest Corner of Washington State including Longview and Vancouver; All of Idaho except for Northern Panhandle	111 S.W. Columbia, Suite 1010, Portland, OR 97210-5842	(503) 326-3052	(503) 326-5051
PENNSYLVA-NIA	Philadelphia Office	U.S. Custom House, Second & Chestnut Streets, Room 402, Philadelphia, PA 19106	(215) 597-4950	(215) 597-4949
PENNSYLVA-NIA	Pittsburgh Office	1000 Liberty Avenue, Room 313, Pittsburgh, PA 15222	(412) 395-4996	(412) 395-5772
PENNSYLVA-NIA	Wilkes-Barre Office	20 N. Pennsylvania Avenue, Wilkes-Barre, PA 18701-3594	(717) 826-6316	(717) 821-4186
RHODE ISLAND	Entire State	See Hartford, Connecticut		
SOUTH CAROLINA	Entire State	Federal Building, 1835 Assembly Street, Room 1072, Columbia, SC 29201-2449	(803) 765-5981	(803) 253-3003
SOUTH DAKOTA	Entire State	See Denver, Colorado		
TENNESSEE	Entire State	1321 Murfreesboro Pike, Suite 511, Nashville, TN 37217-2626	(615) 781-5344	(615) 781-5347

STATE	DISTRICT	ADDRESS	TELEPHONE	FAX
TEXAS	Dallas Office	A. Maceo Smith Federal Building, 525 South Griffin Street, Room 507, Dallas, TX 75202-5007	(214) 767-6294	(214) 767-3839
TEXAS	Houston Office	2320 LaBranch, Room 2100, Houston, TX 77004	(713) 718-3682	(713) 718-3688
TEXAS	San Antonio Office	10127 Morocco, Suite 140, San Antonio, TX 78216	(210) 229-4515	(210) 229-4518
TEXAS	West Texas - Panhandle including Amarillo, Big Spring, El Paso,, Lubbock, Midland, and Odessa	See Albuquerque, New Mexico		
UTAH	Entire State; Colorado - West of Divide; Montana; All of Wyoming except Albany and Laramie Counties	10 West Broadway, Suite 307, Salt Lake City UT 84101	(801) 524-5706	(801) 524-5722
VERMONT	Entire State	See Manchester, New Hampshire		
VIRGINIA	Northern VA	See Baltimore, Maryland		
VIRGINIA	Southwestern VA	See Charleston, West Virginia		
VIRGINIA	Remainder of State	700 East Franklin Street, Suite 560, Richmond, VA 23219	(804) 771-2995	(804) 771-8127

STATE	DISTRICT	ADDRESS	TELEPHONE	FAX
WASHINGTON	All of Washington State except for areas covered by Portland, Oregon office; Alaska; and Northern Panhandle of Idaho including Coeur d'Alene and Lewiston	1111 Third Avenue, Suite 755, Seattle, WA 98101-3212	(206) 553-4482	(206) 553-2883
WEST VIRGINIA	Eastern Panhandle	See Baltimore, Maryland		
WEST VIRGINIA	Remainder of State; Southern Virginia	2 Hale Street, Suite 301, Charleston, WV 25301	(304) 347-5206	(304) 347-5467
WISCONSIN	Entire State	212 East Washington Avenue, Room 309, Madison, WI 53703-2878	(608) 264-5221	(608) 264-5224
WYOMING	Albany and Laramie Counties	See Denver, Colorado		
WYOMING	Remainder of State	See Salt Lake City, Utah		

APPENDIX 5:
DIRECTORY OF THE OCCUPATIONAL SAFETY
AND HEALTH ADMINISTRATION CONSULTATION OFFICES

JURISDICTION	ADDRESS	TELEPHONE	FAX
Alabama	432 Martha Parham West, P.O. Box 870388, Tuscaloosa, AL 35487	205-348-7138	205-348-3049
Alaska	3301 Eagle Street, P.O. Box 107022, Anchorage, AL 99510	907-269-4954	907-269-4950
Arizona	800 West Washington, Phoenix, AZ 85007	602-542-5795	602-542-1614
Arkansas	10421 West Markham, Little Rock, AR 72205	501-682-4522	501-682-4532
California	455 Golden Gate Avenue, Room 5246, San Francisco, CA 94102	415-703-4441	415-972-8513
Colorado	110 Veterinary Science Building, Fort Collins, CO 80523	303-491-6151	303-491-7778
Connecticut	200 Folly Brook Boulevard, Wethersfield, CT 06109	203-566-4550	203-566-6916
Delaware	4425 Market Street, Wilmington DE 19802	302-761-8219	302-761-6601
District of Columbia	950 Upshur Street N.W., Washington, DC 20011	202-576-6339	202-576-7282
Florida	2002 St. Augustine Road, Building E, Suite 45, Tallahassee, FL 32399	904-488-3044	904-922-4538
Georgia	Georgia Institute of Technology, O'Keefe Building, Room 22, Atlanta, GA 30332	404-894-2646	404-894-8275
Guam	P.O. Box 9970, Tamuning, Guam 96931	671-475-0126	671-477-2988
Hawaii	830 Punchbowl Street, Honolulu, HI 96813	808-586-9100	808-586-9099
Idaho	1910 University Drive, Boise, ID 83725	208-385-3283	208-385-4411

JURISDICTION	ADDRESS	TELEPHONE	FAX
Illinois	State of Illinois Center, 100 West Randolph Street, Suite 3-400, Chicago, IL 60601	312-814-2337	312-814-7238
Indiana	402 West Washington, Indianapolis, IN 46204	317-232-2688	317-2320748
Iowa	1000 East Grand Avenue, Des Moines, IA 50319	515-281-5352	515-281-4831
Kansas	512 South West 6th Street, Topeka, KS 66603	913-296-7476	913-206-1775
Kentucky	1049 U.S. Highway 127 South, Frankfort, KY 40601	502-564-6895	502-564-4769
Louisiana	P.O. Box 94094, Baton Rouge, LA 70804	504-342-9601	504-342-5158
Maine	State House Station #82, Augusta, ME 04333	207-624-6460	207-624-6449
Maryland	501 St. Paul Place, 3rd Floor, Baltimore, MD 21202	410-333-4210	410-333-8308
Massachusetts	1001 Watertown Street, West Newton, Massachusetts 02165	617-969-7177	617-969-4581
Michigan	3423 North Martin Luther King Boulevard, Lansing, MI 48909	517-335-8250	517-335-8010
Minnesota	443 Lafayette Road, Saint Paul, MN 55155	612-297-2393	612-297-1953
Mississippi	2906 North State Street, Suite 201, Jackson, MS 39216	601-987-3981	601-987-3890
Missouri	3315 West Truman Boulevard, Jefferson City, MO 65109	573-751-3403	573-751-3721
Montana	P.O. Box 1728, Helena, MT 59624	406-444-6418	406-444-4140
Nebraska	State Office Building, 301 Centennial Mall South, Lower Level, Lincoln, NE 68509	402-471-4717	402-471-5039

JURISDICTION	ADDRESS	TELEPHONE	FAX
Nevada	2500 West Washington, Las Vegas, NV 89106	702-486-5016	702-486-5331
New Hampshire	6 Hazen Drive, Concord, NH 03301	603-271-2024	603-271-2667
New Jersey	Station Plaza 4, CN953, 22 South Clinton Avenue, Trenton, NJ 08625	609-292-2424	609-292-4409
New Mexico	525 Camino de Los Marquez, Suite 3, P.O. Box 26110, Santa Fe, NM 87502	505-827-4230	505-827-4422
New York	State Office Campus, Building 12, Room 457, Albany, NY 12240	518-457-2481	518-457-5545
North Carolina	319 Chapanoke Road, Suite 105, Raleigh, NC 27603	919-662-4644	919-662-4671
North Dakota	1200 Missouri Avenue, Room 304, Bismarck, ND 58506	701-328-5188	701-328-5200
Ohio	145 S. Front Street, Columbus, OH 43216	614-644-2246	614-644-3133
Oklahoma	4001 North Lincoln Boulevard, Oklahoma City, OK 73105	405-528-1500	405-528-5751
Oregon	350 Winter Street NE, Room 430, Salem, OR 97310	503-378-3272	503-378-5729
Pennsylvania	Indiana University of Pennsylvania, Safety Sciences Department, 205 Uhler Hall, Indiana, PA 15705	412-357-2561	412-357-2385
Puerto Rico	505 Munoz Rivera Avenue, Hato Rey, PR 00918	809-754-2188	809-767-6051
Rhode Island	3 Capital Hill, Providence, RI 02908	401-277-2438	401-277-6953
South Carolina	3600 Forest Drive, P.O. Box 11329, Columbia, SC 29211	803-734-9614	803-734-9741

JURISDICTION	ADDRESS	TELEPHONE	FAX
South Dakota	South Dakota State University, West Hall, Box 510, 907 Harvey Dunn Street, Brookings, SD 57007	605-688-4101	605-688-6290
Tennessee	710 James Robertson Parkway, 3rd Floor, Nashville, TN 37243	615-741-7036	615-741-3325
Texas	4000 South I H 35, Austin, TX 78704	512-440-3834	512-440-3831
Utah	160 East 300 South, Salt Lake City, UT 84114	801-530-6868	801-530-6992
Vermont	National Life Building, Drawer 20, Montpelier, VT 05602	802-828-2765	802-828-2748
Virginia	13 South 13th Street, Richmond, VA 23219	804-786-6539	804-786-8418
Virgin Islands	3021 Golden Rock, Christiansted, St. Croix, VI 00840	809-772-1315	809-772-4233
Washington	P.O. Box 44643, Olympia, WA 98504	360-902-5638	360-902-5459
West Virginia	Capitol Complex Building #3, 1800 East Washington Street, Room 319, Charleston, WV 25305	304-558-7890	304-558-3797
Wisconsin	1414 East Washington Avenue, Madison, WI 53703	608-266-8579	608-266-9711
Wyoming	Herschler Building 2 East, 122 West 25th Street, Cheyenne, WY 82008	307-777-7786	307-777-3646

APPENDIX 6:
THE FAMILY AND MEDICAL LEAVE ACT OF 1993

SECTION 1. SHORT TITLE; TABLE OF CONTENTS.

(a) SHORT TITLE.—This Act may be cited as the "Family and Medical Leave Act of 1993".

(b) TABLE OF CONTENTS.—(Omitted)

SECTION 2. FINDINGS AND PURPOSES.

(a) FINDINGS.—Congress finds that—

(1) the number of single-parent households and two-parent households in which the single parent or both parents work is increasing significantly;

(2) it is important for the development of children and the family unit that fathers and mothers be able to participate in early childrearing and the care of family members who have serious health conditions;

(3) the lack of employment policies to accommodate working parents can force individuals to choose between job security and parenting;

(4) there is inadequate job security for employees who have serious health conditions that prevent them from working for temporary periods;

(5) due to the nature of the roles of men and women in our society, the primary responsibility for family caretaking often falls on women, and such responsibility affects the working lives of women more than it affects the working lives of men; and

(6) employment standards that apply to one gender only have serious potential for encouraging employers to discriminate against employees and applicants for employment who are of that gender.

(b) PURPOSES.—It is the purpose of this Act—

(1) to balance the demands of the workplace with the needs of families, to promote the stability and economic security of families, and to promote national interests in preserving family integrity;

(2) to entitle employees to take reasonable leave for medical reasons, for the birth or adoption of a child, and for the care of a child, spouse, or parent who has a serious health condition;

(3) to accomplish the purposes described in paragraphs (1) and (2) in a manner that accommodates the legitimate interests of employers;

(4) to accomplish the purposes described in paragraphs (1) and (2) in a manner that, consistent with the Equal Protection Clause of the Fourteenth Amendment, minimizes the potential for employment discrimination on the basis of sex by ensuring generally that leave is available for eligible medical reasons (including maternity-related disability) and for compelling family reasons, on a gender-neutral basis; and

TITLE I—GENERAL REQUIREMENTS FOR LEAVE

DEFINITIONS

As used in this title:

(1) COMMERCE.—The terms "commerce" and "industry or activity affecting commerce" mean any activity, business, or industry in commerce or in which a labor dispute would hinder or obstruct commerce or the free flow of commerce, and include "commerce" and any "industry affecting commerce", as defined in paragraphs (1) and (3) of section 501 of the Labor Management Relations Act, 1947 (29 U.S.C. 142 (1) and (3)).

(2) ELIGIBLE EMPLOYEE.—

(A) IN GENERAL.—The term "eligible employee" means an employee who has been employed—

(i) for at least 12 months by the employer with respect to whom leave is requested under section 102; and

(ii) for at least 1,250 hours of service with such employer during the previous 12-month period.

(B) EXCLUSIONS.—The term "eligible employee" does not include—

(i) any Federal officer or employee covered under subchapter V of chapter 63 of title 5, United States Code (as added by title II of this Act); or

(ii) any employee of an employer who is employed at a worksite at which such employer employs less than 50 employees if the total number of employees employed by that employer within 75 miles of that worksite is less than 50.

(C) DETERMINATION.—For purposes of determining whether an employee meets the hours of service requirement specified in subparagraph (A)(ii), the legal standards established under section 7 of the Fair Labor Standards Act of 1938 (29 U.S.C. 207) shall apply.

(3) EMPLOY; EMPLOYEE; STATE.—The terms "employ", "employee", and "State" have the same meanings given such terms in subsections (c), (e), and (g) of section 3 of the Fair Labor Standards Act of 1938 (29 U.S.C. 203(c), (e), and (g)).

(4) EMPLOYER.—

(A) IN GENERAL.—The term "employer"—

(i) means any person engaged in commerce or in any industry or activity affecting commerce who employs 50 or more employees for each working day during each of 20 or more calendar workweeks in the current or preceding calendar year;

(ii) includes—

(I) any person who acts, directly or indirectly, in the interest of an employer to any of the employees of such employer; and

(II) any successor in interest of an employer; and

(iii) includes any "public agency", as defined in section 3(x) of the Fair Labor Standards Act of 1938 (29 U.S.C. 203(x)).

(B) PUBLIC AGENCY.—For purposes of subparagraph (A)(iii), a public agency shall be considered to be a person engaged in commerce or in an industry or activity affecting commerce.

(5) EMPLOYMENT BENEFITS.—The term "employment benefits" means all benefits provided or made available to employees by an employer, including group life insurance, health insurance, disability insurance, sick leave, annual leave, educational benefits, and pensions, regardless of whether such benefits are provided by a practice or written policy of an employer or through an "employee benefit plan", as defined in section 3(3) of the Employee Retirement Income Security Act of 1974 (29 U.S.C. 1002(3)).

(6) HEALTH CARE PROVIDER.—The term "health care provider" means—

(A) a doctor of medicine or osteopathy who is authorized to practice medicine or surgery (as appropriate) by the State in which the doctor practices; or

(B) any other person determined by the Secretary to be capable of providing health care services.

(7) PARENT.—The term "parent" means the biological parent of an employee or an individual who stood in loco parentis to an employee when the employee was a son or daughter.

(8) PERSON.—The term "person" has the same meaning given such term in section 3(a) of the Fair Labor Standards Act of 1938 (29 U.S.C. 203(a)).

(9) REDUCED LEAVE SCHEDULE.—The term "reduced leave schedule" means a leave schedule that reduces the usual number of hours per workweek, or hours per workday, of an employee.

(10) SECRETARY.—The term "Secretary" means the Secretary of Labor.

(11) SERIOUS HEALTH CONDITION.—The term "serious health condition" means an illness, injury, impairment, or physical or mental condition that involves—

(A) inpatient care in a hospital, hospice, or residential medical care facility; or

(B) continuing treatment by a health care provider.

(12) SON OR DAUGHTER.—The term "son or daughter" means a biological, adopted, or foster child, a stepchild, a legal ward, or a child of a person standing in loco parentis, who is—

(A) under 18 years of age; or

(B) 18 years of age or older and incapable of self-care because of a ental or physical disability.

(13) SPOUSE.—The term "spouse" means a husband or wife, as the case may be.

SECTION 102. LEAVE REQUIREMENT.

(a) IN GENERAL.—

(1) ENTITLEMENT TO LEAVE.—Subject to section 103, an eligible employee shall be entitled to a total of 12 workweeks of leave during any 12-month period for one or more of the following:

(A) Because of the birth of a son or daughter of the employee and in order to care for such son or daughter.

(B) Because of the placement of a son or daughter with the employee for adoption or foster care.

(C) In order to care for the spouse, or a son, daughter, or parent, of the employee, if such spouse, son, daughter, or parent has a serious health condition.

(D) Because of a serious health condition that makes the employee unable to perform the functions of the position of such employee.

(2) EXPIRATION OF ENTITLEMENT.—The entitlement to leave under subparagraphs (A) and (B) of paragraph (1) for a birth or placement of a son or daughter shall expire at the end of the 12-month period beginning on the date of such birth or placement.

(b) LEAVE TAKEN INTERMITTENTLY OR ON A REDUCED LEAVE SCHEDULE.—

(1) IN GENERAL.—Leave under subparagraph (A) or (B) of subsection (a)(1) shall not be taken by an employee intermittently or on a reduced leave schedule unless the employee and the employer of the employee agree otherwise. Subject to paragraph (2), subsection (e)(2), and section 103(b)(5), leave under subparagraph (C) or (D) of subsection (a)(1) may be taken intermittently or on a reduced leave schedule when medically necessary. The taking of leave intermittently or on a reduced leave schedule pursuant to this paragraph shall not result in a reduction in the total amount of leave to which the employee is entitled under subsection (a) beyond the amount of leave actually taken.

(2) ALTERNATIVE POSITION.—If an employee requests intermittent leave, or leave on a reduced leave schedule, under subparagraph (C) or (D) of subsection (a)(1), that is foreseeable based on planned medical treatment, the employer may require such employee to transfer temporarily to an available alternative position offered by the employer for which the employee is qualified and that—

(A) has equivalent pay and benefits; and

(B) better accommodates recurring periods of leave than the regular employment position of the employee.

(c) UNPAID LEAVE PERMITTED.—Except as provided in subsection (d), leave granted under subsection (a) may consist of unpaid leave. Where an employee is otherwise exempt under regulations issued by the Secretary pursuant to section 13(a)(1) of the Fair Labor Standards Act of 1938 (29 U.S.C. 213(a)(1)), the compliance of an employer with this title by providing unpaid leave shall not affect the exempt status of the employee under such section.

(d) RELATIONSHIP TO PAID LEAVE.—

(1) UNPAID LEAVE.—If an employer provides paid leave for fewer than 12 workweeks, the additional weeks of leave necessary to attain the

12 workweeks of leave required under this title may be provided without compensation.

(2) SUBSTITUTION OF PAID LEAVE.—

(A) IN GENERAL.—An eligible employee may elect, or an employer may require the employee, to substitute any of the accrued paid vacation leave, personal leave, or family leave of the employee for leave provided under subparagraph (A), (B), or (C) of subsection (a)(1) for any part of the 12-week period of such leave under such subsection.

(B) SERIOUS HEALTH CONDITION.—An eligible employee may elect, or an employer may require the employee, to substitute any of the accrued paid vacation leave, personal leave, or medical or sick leave of the employee for leave provided under subparagraph (C) or (D) of subsection (a)(1) for any part of the 12-week period of such leave under such subsection, except that nothing in this title shall require an employer to provide paid sick leave or paid medical leave in any situation in which such employer would not normally provide any such paid leave.

(e) FORESEEABLE LEAVE.—

(1) REQUIREMENT OF NOTICE.—In any case in which the necessity for leave under subparagraph (A) or (B) of subsection (a)(1) is foreseeable based on an expected birth or placement, the employee shall provide the employer with not less than 30 days' notice, before the date the leave is to begin, of the employee's intention to take leave under such subparagraph, except that if the date of the birth or placement requires leave to begin in less than 30 days, the employee shall provide such notice as is practicable.

(2) DUTIES OF EMPLOYEE.—In any case in which the necessity for leave under subparagraph (C) or (D) of subsection (a)(1) is foreseeable based on planned medical treatment, the employee—

(A) shall make a reasonable effort to schedule the treatment so as not to disrupt unduly the operations of the employer, subject to the approval of the health care provider of the employee or the health care provider of the son, daughter, spouse, or parent of the employee, as appropriate; and

(B) shall provide the employer with not less than 30 days' notice, before the date the leave is to begin, of the employee's intention to take leave under such subparagraph, except that if the date of the treatment requires leave to begin in less than 30 days, the employee shall provide such notice as is practicable.

(f) SPOUSES EMPLOYED BY THE SAME EMPLOYER.—In any case in which a husband and wife entitled to leave under subsection (a) are employed by the same employer, the aggregate number of workweeks of leave to which both may be entitled may be limited to 12 workweeks during any 12-month period, if such leave is taken—

(1) under subparagraph (A) or (B) of subsection (a)(1); or

(2) to care for a sick parent under subparagraph (C) of such subsection.

SECTION 103. CERTIFICATION.

(a) IN GENERAL.—An employer may require that a request for leave under subparagraph (C) or (D) of section 102(a)(1) be supported by a certification issued by the health care provider of the eligible employee or of the son, daughter, spouse, or parent of the employee, as appropriate. The employee shall provide, in a timely manner, a copy of such certification to the employer.

(b) SUFFICIENT CERTIFICATION.—Certification provided under subsection (a) shall be sufficient if it states—

(1) the date on which the serious health condition commenced;

(2) the probable duration of the condition;

(3) the appropriate medical facts within the knowledge of the health care provider regarding the condition;

(4)(A) for purposes of leave under section 102(a)(1)(C), a statement that the eligible employee is needed to care for the son, daughter, spouse, or parent and an estimate of the amount of time that such employee is needed to care for the son, daughter, spouse, or parent; and

(B) for purposes of leave under section 102(a)(1)(D), a statement that the employee is unable to perform the functions of the position of the employee;

(5) in the case of certification for intermittent leave, or leave on a reduced leave schedule, for planned medical treatment, the dates on which such treatment is expected to be given and the duration of such treatment;

(6) in the case of certification for intermittent leave, or leave on a reduced leave schedule, under section 102(a)(1)(D), a statement of the medical necessity for the intermittent leave or leave on a reduced leave

schedule, and the expected duration of the intermittent leave or reduced leave schedule; and

(7) in the case of certification for intermittent leave, or leave on a re-duced leave schedule, under section 102(a)(1)(C), a statement that the employee's intermittent leave or leave on a reduced leave schedule is necessary for the care of the son, daughter, parent, or spouse who has a serious health condition, or will assist in their recovery, and the expected duration and schedule of the intermittent leave or reduced leave sched-ule.

(c) SECOND OPINION.—

(1) IN GENERAL.—In any case in which the employer has reason to doubt the validity of the certification provided under subsection (a) for leave under subparagraph (C) or (D) of section 102(a)(1), the employer may require, at the expense of the employer, that the eligible employee obtain the opinion of a second health care provider designated or ap-proved by the employer concerning any information certified under sub-section (b) for such leave.

(2) LIMITATION.—A health care provider designated or approved under paragraph (1) shall not be employed on a regular basis by the em-ployer.

(d) RESOLUTION OF CONFLICTING OPINIONS.—

(1) IN GENERAL.—In any case in which the second opinion de-scribed in subsection (c) differs from the opinion in the original certifi-cation provided under subsection (a), the employer may require, at the expense of the employer, that the employee obtain the opinion of a third health care provider designated or approved jointly by the employer and the employee concerning the information certified under subsection (b).

(2) FINALITY.—The opinion of the third health care provider con-cerning the information certified under subsection (b) shall be consid-ered to be final and shall be binding on the employer and the employee.

(e) SUBSEQUENT RECERTIFICATION.—The employer may require that the eligible employee obtain subsequent recertifications on a reason-able basis.

SECTION 104. EMPLOYMENT AND BENEFITS PROTECTION.

(a) RESTORATION TO POSITION.—

(1) IN GENERAL.—Except as provided in subsection (b), any eligible employee who takes leave under section 102 for the intended purpose of the leave shall be entitled, on return from such leave—

(A) to be restored by the employer to the position of employment held by the employee when the leave commenced; or

(B) to be restored to an equivalent position with equivalent employment benefits, pay, and other terms and conditions of employment.

(2) LOSS OF BENEFITS.—The taking of leave under section 102 shall not result in the loss of any employment benefit accrued prior to the date on which the leave commenced.

(3) LIMITATIONS.—Nothing in this section shall be construed to entitle any restored employee to—

(A) the accrual of any seniority or employment benefits during any period of leave; or

(B) any right, benefit, or position of employment other than any right, benefit, or position to which the employee would have been entitled had the employee not taken the leave.

(4) CERTIFICATION.—As a condition of restoration under paragraph (1) for an employee who has taken leave under section 102(a)(1)(D), the employer may have a uniformly applied practice or policy that requires each such employee to receive certification from the health care provider of the employee that the employee is able to resume work, except that nothing in this paragraph shall supersede a valid State or local law or a collective bargaining agreement that governs the return to work of such employees.

(5) CONSTRUCTION.—Nothing in this subsection shall be construed to prohibit an employer from requiring an employee on leave under section 102 to report periodically to the employer on the status and intention of the employee to return to work.

(b) EXEMPTION CONCERNING CERTAIN HIGHLY COMPENSATED EMPLOYEES.—

(1) DENIAL OF RESTORATION.—An employer may deny restoration under subsection (a) to any eligible employee described in paragraph (2) if—

(A) such denial is necessary to prevent substantial and grievous economic injury to the operations of the employer;

(B) the employer notifies the employee of the intent of the employer to deny restoration on such basis at the time the employer determines that such injury would occur; and

(C) in any case in which the leave has commenced, the employee elects not to return to employment after receiving such notice.

(2) AFFECTED EMPLOYEES.—An eligible employee described in paragraph (1) is a salaried eligible employee who is among the highest paid 10 percent of the employees employed by the employer within 75 miles of the facility at which the employee is employed.

(c) MAINTENANCE OF HEALTH BENEFITS.—

(1) COVERAGE.—Except as provided in paragraph (2), during any period that an eligible employee takes leave under section 102, the employer shall maintain coverage under any "group health plan" (as defined in section 5000(b)(1) of the Internal Revenue Code of 1986) for the duration of such leave at the level and under the conditions coverage would have been provided if the employee had continued in employment continuously for the duration of such leave.

(2) FAILURE TO RETURN FROM LEAVE.—The employer may recover the premium that the employer paid for maintaining coverage for the employee under such group health plan during any period of unpaid leave under section 102 if—

(A) the employee fails to return from leave under section 102 after the period of leave to which the employee is entitled has expired; and

(B) the employee fails to return to work for a reason other than—

(i) the continuation, recurrence, or onset of a serious health condition that entitles the employee to leave under subparagraph (C) or (D) of section 102(a)(1); or

(ii) other circumstances beyond the control of the employee.

(3) CERTIFICATION.—

(A) ISSUANCE.—An employer may require that a claim that an employee is unable to return to work because of the continuation, recurrence, or onset of the serious health condition described in paragraph (2)(B)(i) be supported by—

(i) a certification issued by the health care provider of the son, daughter, spouse, or parent of the employee, as appropriate, in the case of an employee unable to return to work because of a condition specified in section 102(a)(1)(C); or

(ii) a certification issued by the health care provider of the eligible employee, in the case of an employee unable to return to work because of a condition specified in section 102(a)(1)(D).

(B) COPY.—The employee shall provide, in a timely manner, a copy of such certification to the employer.

(C) SUFFICIENCY OF CERTIFICATION.—

(i) LEAVE DUE TO SERIOUS HEALTH CONDITION OF EMPLOYEE.—The certification described in subparagraph (A)(ii) shall be sufficient if the certification states that a serious health condition prevented the employee from being able to perform the functions of the position of the employee on the date that the leave of the employee expire.

(ii) LEAVE DUE TO SERIOUS HEALTH CONDITION OF FAMILY MEMBER.—The certification described in subparagraph (A)(i) shall be sufficient if the certification states that the employee is needed to care for the son, daughter, spouse, or parent who has a serious health condition on the date that the leave of the employee expired.

SECTION 105. PROHIBITED ACTS.

(a) INTERFERENCE WITH RIGHTS.—

(1) EXERCISE OF RIGHTS.—It shall be unlawful for any employer to interfere with, restrain, or deny the exercise of or the attempt to exercise, any right provided under this title.

(2) DISCRIMINATION.—It shall be unlawful for any employer to discharge or in any other manner discriminate against any individual for opposing any practice made unlawful by this title.

(b) INTERFERENCE WITH PROCEEDINGS OR INQUIRIES.—It shall be unlawful for any person to discharge or in any other manner discriminate against any individual because such individual—

(1) has filed any charge, or has instituted or caused to be instituted any proceeding, under or related to this title;

(2) has given, or is about to give, any information in connection with any inquiry or proceeding relating to any right provided under this title; or

(3) has testified, or is about to testify, in any inquiry or proceeding relating to any right provided under this title.

GLOSSARY

GLOSSARY

Age Discrimination in Employment Act (ADEA) - A federal law which provides that workers over the age of 40 cannot be arbitrarily discriminated against because of age in connection with any employment decision.

American Civil Liberties Union (ACLU) - A nationwide organization dedicated to the enforcement and preservation of rights and civil liberties guaranteed by the federal and state constitutions.

Americans with Disabilities Act (ADA) - A federal law which prohibits employers from discriminating on the basis of a "qualified" disability as set forth in the statute.

Back Pay - Wages awarded to an employee who was illegally discharged.

Base Rate Pay - An employee's basic hourly rate excluding overtime.

Blue-Collar Workers - Generally refers to individuals engaged in manual labor.

Boycott - A means of exerting pressure on a particular business by refusing to buy its goods or services.

Bureau of Labor Statistics - A division of the U.S. Department of Labor that complies statistics related to employment.

Consolidated Omnibus Budget Reconciliation Act (COBRA) -Federal law which extends a terminated employee's health insurance coverage at group rates for a specified period of time following termination.

Compensatory Time - Leave time given to an employee in lieu of premium pay for overtime work.

Consumer Price Index - A monthly statistical study of the retail prices of certain consumer items and services prepared by the Bureau of Labor Statistics.

Cost of Living Allowance - An increase in wages which is based on an increase in the cost of living.

Davis-Bacon Act - A federal statute which sets forth the wages that contractors must pay certain employees who work on federally funded construction projects.

Defamation - An libelous (written) or slanderous (spoken) statement which maligns the character of another.

Double Time - Premium pay rate that is twice the employee's basic rate of pay.

Employee Retirement Income Security Act of 1974 (ERISA) - A federal statute which governs the administration of pension plans.

Fair Labor Standards Act (FLSA) - Federal law governing federal wage and hour regulations.

Federal Unemployment Tax Act - Federal law which taxes employers for the purpose of funding the unemployment compensation program.

Independent Contractor - An individual who contracts to perform services for others without qualifying legally as an employee.

Jones Act - The federal statute permitting a seaman, or a representative, the right to sue for personal injuries suffered in the course of the seaman's employment.

Labor Organization - An association of workers for the purpose of bargaining the terms and conditions of employment on behalf of labor and management.

Labor Dispute - A conflict between a union and an employer.

Layoff - A forced furlough from employment, on a temporary basis, generally caused by a lack of available work.

National Labor Relations Act - A federal statute known as the Wagner Act of 1935 and amended by the Taft-Hartley Act of 1947, which established the National Labor Relations Board to regulate the relations between employers and employees.

National Labor Relations Board - An independent agency created by the National Labor Relations Act of 1935 (Wagner Act), as amended by the acts of 1947 (Taft-Hartley Act) and 1959 (Landrum-Griffin Act), established to regulate the relations between employers and employees.

National Mediation Board - Organization created by Congress in 1934, amending the Railway Labor Act, for the purpose of mediating disputes over wages, hours and working conditions which arise between rail and air carriers, and their employees.

Payroll Deduction - Money held from a worker's salary which is allocated to certain obligations, such as income taxes, union dues, health plan benefits, etc.

Payroll Period - The length of time between paydays.

Pension Plan - A retirement plan established by an employer for the payment of pension benefits to employees upon retirement.

Polygraph - A lie detector test.

Premium Pay - Wages paid to an employee above the basic pay rate, e.g. overtime pay.

Quid Pro Quo - Latin for "something for something." Refers to the exchange of promises or performances between two parties. Also refers to the legal consideration necessary to create a binding contract.

Reinstatement - Refers to the return of an employee to employment from which he or she was illegally dismissed.

Severance Pay - Monies paid to a terminated employee.

Shift - Refers to an employee's regular work hours.

Shift Differential - Premium pay earned by an employee who works an unusual or inconvenient shift, e.g. night shift.

Straight Time Pay - Wages paid to an employee for working his or her regular hours.

Sweat Shop - A business which employs workers under poor working conditions at extremely low wages.

Taft-Hartley Act - Refers to the Labor-Management Relations Act of 1947, which was established to prescribe the legitimate rights of both employees and employers.

Take-Home Pay - Net wages paid to an employee after all applicable deductions are subtracted.

Temporary Employee - An employee who is hired to work on a short-term basis.

Termination - Refers to cessation of employment, e.g. by quitting or dismissal.

Unfair Labor Practice - Any activities carried out by either a union or an employer which violate the National Labor Relations Act.

Union Shop - A workplace where all of the employees are members of a union.

Vacation - Authorized leave from work, with or without pay.

Wages - Compensation paid to an employee.

Whistleblower - An employee who reports on violations of the law which occur in the workplace.

White Collar Workers - Generally refers to individuals engaged in office work.

Wildcat Strike - An unauthorized strike for which the union representing the workers disclaims responsibility.

Wrongful Discharge - An unlawful dismissal of an employee.

Zone of Employment - The physical area in which injuries to an employee are covered by worker compensation laws.

BIBLIOGRAPHY

BIBLIOGRAPHY AND ADDITIONAL READING

Black's Law Dictionary, Fifth Edition. St. Paul, MN: West Publishing Company, 1979.

Feliu, Alfred, G., *Primer on Individual Employee Rights.* Washington, DC: The Bureau of National Affairs, Inc., 1996.

Hunt, James W., *The Law of the Workplace: Rights of Employers and Employees.* Washington, DC: The Bureau of National Affairs, Inc., 1988.

Joel, Lewin G. III, *Every Employee's Guide to the Law.* New York, NY: Pantheon Books, 1993.